Meze Cooking

Red sky at night, shepherd's delight . . . Hóra Sfakion at dusk.

Meze
Cooking

Easy-to-follow Recipes to Make
Delicious Mediterranean Snacks

Sarah Maxwell

APPLE

A QUINTET BOOK

This edition published in 2000 by
Apple Press
Sheridan House
112-116A Western Road
Hove
East Sussex BN3 1DD

Copyright © 2000 Quintet Publishing Ltd.

ISBN 1-84092-257-5
Reprinted 2002, 2003, 2004
All rights reserved.

This book was designed and produced by
Quintet Publishing Ltd
6 Blundell Street
London N7 9BH

Creative Director: Richard Dewing
Designer: Chris Dymond
Project Editor: Damian Thompson
Editor: Diana Vowles
Illustrator: Marianna Ziffo
Photographer: Trevor Wood

Manufactured in Hong Kong by
Regent Publishing Services Limited
Printed in China by
Midas Printing International Limited

Contents

Introduction

Meze is perhaps the most famous feature of Greek cuisine and, although the spelling may vary, its meaning is always the same. The Meze is a titbit of food, a small serving of something delicious to accompany a glass of something cool as you sit back and relax in the Mediterranean sunshine, chatting away to friends and passers-by.

In Greece, Meze is served at every café, in every house and on many a street corner. It can be anything from a small nibble of toasted pumpkin seeds to a whole array of tempting salads, pulse dishes, dips, tiny kebabs, vegetables – stuffed and unstuffed – and much, much more, creating a mass of colour, tastes and textures, all chosen to complement and enhance each other.

If you, like me, are one of those people who finds it difficult to choose from a menu or to decide what to cook for a special occasion, then Meze is the answer to your prayers. A little bit of everything keeps you satisfied and your guests interested as the myriad of dishes flow from the kitchen until you couldn't possibly take any more . . . well, maybe just one more!

This book provides you with an extensive range of dishes to serve at the Meze table. Some of the recipes are traditional, others classic, and still more are adaptations with the use of a little poetic licence, whereby substitutions for ingredients or changes in methods of cooking have occasionally been made so that the recipes are more accessible to you.

Create your own Meze table by choosing your favourite selection of dishes from the chapters which follow, or try one of the suggested occasion menus which appear now and then throughout the book. Serve the dishes a few at a time, starting with the hors-d'oeuvre Meze, followed by the main course dishes and finishing with the sweet Meze.

Of course, you needn't restrict these recipes to the authentic Meze table. Any one of them can be added to a menu, prepared for a light lunch, served as a starter or a dessert, whenever you feel like adding a taste of Greece to the occasion. You may want to increase the quantities of ingredients if, say, one Meze dish is to be served as a main course on its own (remember to allow for extra cooking time too). That's the wonderful thing about Greek Meze cooking – you can always add a little extra of one thing or another if you have a sudden unexpected guest arrive, or you simply want the dish to stretch a little bit further.

Meze cooking exemplifies the Greek way of life – it's relaxed in every aspect. There is no particular way to serve most Meze dishes; you simply pick and choose the ones you like best and lay them out for one and all to help themselves. Most of the dishes can be prepared in advance, others can be left to simmer or be reheated just before serving – so whatever the occasion, with Greek Meze food you'll be sure to have plenty of time to enjoy its preparation.

LEFT
En route to the vegetable market at Heraklion . . . fruit, along with tobacco, textiles and olive oil, is among the country's biggest exports.

FACING PAGE
The palace of Knossos on Crete, centre of the Minoan civilization in 2,000 BC. According to legend, it was here that Theseus encountered the Minotaur.

A Word about Wine

Greece is home to more than 300 native grape varieties and the country produces a surprising array of full-bodied velvety reds, some excellent dessert wines and a wide range of whites and rosés.

Retsina is perhaps the most famous and widely known Greek wine. Most non-Greeks who try it for the first time find its mysterious flavour one for the taste to acquire. It is made in exactly the same way as all white wines, except that a little pine resin is added at the start of fermentation, giving it that very distinctive flavour. Retsina should be drunk young and chilled and is a perfect accompaniment to Greek food in general.

Naoussa and Naoussa Grande Reserve are two notable wines from the Macedonian wine-growing region of Greece. These wines are excellent dry robust reds which are aged for at least four years before they are at their best. Saved for a slightly special occasion, these wines should be served at room temperature with rich-tasting savoury recipes.

The white Muscat grape dominates the Greek island of Samos, which was one of the first wine-growing regions of Greece. The pale gold Muscat of Samos is one of the best-known wines in all of Greece. This light, crisp, sweet white wine should be served chilled and is suitable as an accompaniment to fish or white meat dishes as well as being an excellent dessert wine.

Although not a wine, ouzo deserves to be mentioned here, if only because it is the true national drink of Greece. Classified as a spirit, and a potent one at that, this clear, slightly thick, licorice-flavoured liquor is distilled from the residuals of the grape after it has been pressed for wine. Ouzo should be drunk at room temperature, with or without a little iced water, but always with something to eat and in the company of good friends or family.

Gaudy boats enliven Hania's harbour in midsummer.

Hors-d'Oeuvre Meze

Chicken Soup with Egg and Lemon Sauce

Classic Greek Vegetable Soup

Aubergine Dip

Yoghurt, Cucumber and Garlic Dip

Easter Lamb Soup

Cod's Roe Dip

Classic Greek Salad

Greek Potato Salad

Chickpea Dip

Tuna Fish with Chickpeas

Roast Pepper Salad

Marinated Meatballs

Fried Cheese

Chicken Filo Rolls

Crispy Meat-filled Ovals

Cheese Filo Triangles

Mini Kebabs

Chicken Soup with Egg and Lemon Sauce

KOTOSOUPA AVGOLEMONO

◆ ◆ ◆ ◆

This tangy soup is deliciously light and refreshing. It is hearty enough for a winter soup, yet zesty enough to be served in the summer too.

Preparation time: about 30 minutes
Cooking time: about 3½ hours

SERVES: 6

- *1.6 kg/3½ lb oven-ready chicken, without giblets*
- *1 large onion*
- *2.3 l/4 pt water*
- *salt and freshly ground black pepper, to taste*
- *2 cloves*
- *225 g/8 oz long-grain rice*
- *2 eggs*
- *freshly squeezed juice of 1 lemon*

1 Place the chicken in a large saucepan with the onion, cloves and water. Slowly bring the contents of the pan to the boil, skimming off the foam as it appears. Simmer for 2½–3 hours, or until the meat comes away from the bones easily.

2 Remove from the heat. Lift the chicken out of the pan and place on a chopping board. Remove the onion and cloves from the pan with a slotted spoon and discard. Using a carving knife and fork, take the meat off the bones of the chicken and cut or shred into bite-sized pieces. Discard the bones.

3 Return the chicken pieces to the saucepan and gently bring the soup back to the boil. Add the rice, cover the pan and simmer the soup for 15–20 minutes, or until the rice is tender.

4 In a medium-sized bowl, whisk together the eggs and lemon juice until frothy. Add 4–5 ladlefuls of the soup to the egg mixture, whisking vigorously after each addition. Pour the egg mixture into the saucepan and stir continuously with a wooden spoon until evenly combined. Adjust the seasoning, if necessary. Serve immediately.

BELOW
The unparalleled clarity of Mediterranean light lends brilliance to an otherwise ordinary scene like this house façade in Psichró.

Classic Greek Vegetable Soup
HORTOSOUPA

❖ ❖ ❖ ❖

Serve this classic Greek soup with freshly baked Olive Bread (*Eliopitta*).

Preparation time: about 15 minutes
Cooking time: about 1 hour 35 minutes
SERVES: 6–8

- 120 ml/4 fl oz olive oil
- 2 garlic cloves, crushed
- 2 onions, finely chopped
- 225 g/8 oz cabbage, finely shredded
- 3 carrots, chopped
- 3 celery sticks, chopped
- 2 large potatoes, peeled and diced
- 2.3 l/4 pt vegetable stock
- or water
- 4 tomatoes, skinned, seeded and chopped
- salt and freshly ground black pepper, to taste
- 4 tbsp chopped fresh parsley
- 50 g/2 oz feta or kefalotyri cheese, grated

1 Heat the olive oil in a large saucepan and add the garlic and onion. Cook for 5 minutes, until the onion is softened but not coloured. Add the cabbage and continue to cook for another 3–4 minutes.

2 Add the carrots and celery to the saucepan, stir and cook for a further 5 minutes. Add the potatoes, stir and cook gently for another 5 minutes, until the vegetables are softened.

3 Pour in the vegetable stock or water and stir well. Increase the heat to bring the soup to the boil. Cover and simmer for 12–15 minutes. Add the tomato and season to taste with salt and freshly ground black pepper. Re-cover and gently simmer the soup for about 1 hour. Stir in the parsley just before the end of the cooking time. Serve sprinkled with grated cheese.

Aubergine Dip
MELITZANOSALATA

Large, fresh aubergines are needed for this recipe to be sure of a rich, pungent flavour. Serve this dip smooth or with a slightly rougher texture, if you prefer.

Preparation time: about 20 minutes
Cooking time: about 1 hour
Oven temperature: 190°C/375°F/Gas 5
SERVES: 4–6

- 2 large aubergines
- 4 garlic cloves, peeled
- 50 ml/2 fl oz olive oil, plus extra for greasing
- 1 tbsp vinegar
- ½ tsp caster sugar
- salt and freshly ground black pepper, to taste
- finely chopped black olives and finely chopped fresh parsley, to garnish

1 Preheat the oven to 190°C/375°F/Gas 5. Wash the aubergines and pat dry with absorbent kitchen paper. Prick the aubergines all over with a fork and arrange them on a well-greased baking sheet. Bake for about 1 hour, or until the skins are shrivelled and the flesh is soft. Remove from the oven.

2 Allow the aubergines to cool slightly, then peel and cut in half lengthways. Scoop out the inner seeds and discard. Place the aubergine flesh in a food processor or blender with the garlic and purée to combine.

3 With the motor still running, add the oil in a continuous stream, then add the vinegar. Sprinkle in the sugar and season to taste with salt and pepper. Continue to purée until the desired texture is achieved. Transfer the dip to a serving bowl and scatter over the chopped olives and parsley to serve.

Yoghurt, Cucumber and Garlic Dip
TZATZIKI

◇ ◇ ◇ ◇

This light and refreshing dip should always be served well chilled. On its own with fresh pitta bread or as an accompaniment to fritters and other fried foods, it is easy to make and very delicious.

Preparation time: about 10 minutes
Cooking time: none
SERVES: 4–6

- 450 g/1 lb natural yoghurt
- ½ cucumber
- 3 garlic cloves, crushed
- 2 tbsp chopped fresh mint
- 2 tbsp olive oil
- 1 tbsp white wine vinegar
- salt, to taste
- chopped fresh mint, to garnish

1 Place the yoghurt in a medium-sized bowl. Peel and grate the cucumber, squeezing a little at a time in the palm of your hand to remove the excess water. Stir the cucumber into the yoghurt.

2 Stir in the garlic, fresh mint, olive oil and vinegar and season with salt, to taste. Cover and chill in the refrigerator until required. Just before serving, garnish with chopped fresh mint.

Easter Lamb Soup
MAGEIRITSA

◇ ◇ ◇ ◇

Mageiritsa is the Greek word for the Easter meal leftovers. It is traditional for no part of the animal, lamb or goat, to go to waste. Some people even use the feet! This version uses shredded lamb and would be served with Greek Easter Bread (*Tsoureki*) to break the fast after the Midnight Mass. (See page 37 for a traditional Easter menu.)

Preparation time: about 30 minutes
Cooking time: about 3½ hours
SERVES: 6–8

- 1.8 kg/4 lb shoulder of lamb
- 2 celery sticks, chopped
- 1 large carrot, chopped
- 1 large onion, chopped
- salt and freshly ground black pepper, to taste
- 2.3 l/4 pt water
- 4 tbsp chopped fresh dill
- 4 tbsp chopped fresh mint
- 100 g/4 oz long-grain rice
- 3 eggs
- freshly squeezed juice of 1 large lemon
- chopped fresh dill and mint, to garnish

1 Place the lamb in a large saucepan with the celery, carrot and onion. Season and add the water.

2 Bring to the boil and simmer the soup for 2½–3 hours, skimming the foam off the top as it appears, until the meat is tender and comes away from the bone easily.

3 Remove the meat from the saucepan and place on a chopping board. Using a carving knife and fork, cut the meat away from the bone and shred it finely. Return the meat to the saucepan and add the chopped dill and mint and stir in the rice. Bring the soup back to boiling point, stirring occasionally, and simmer until the rice is tender.

4 In a medium-sized bowl, whisk the eggs with the lemon juice. Whisk in 3–4 ladlefuls of the soup, then return the egg mixture to the saucepan, stirring continuously with a wooden spoon, until evenly blended. Serve the soup in individual bowls, garnished with chopped herbs.

Cod's Roe Dip
TARAMOSALATA

Traditionally made with carp's roe, *taramosalata* is often made with cod's roe instead. Although this might change the flavour of the finished dish slightly, it reduces the cost considerably. Cod's roe is also far more readily available.

Preparation time: about 10 minutes
Cooking time: none
SERVES: 4

- 75 g/3 oz carp's or cod's roe, membranes removed
- 1 medium-thick slice of white bread, crusts removed
- 1 medium potato, boiled until soft, and peeled
- 1 onion, finely chopped
- 120 ml/4 fl oz olive oil
- freshly squeezed juice of 1 lemon
- lemon slices and chopped fresh parsley, to garnish

1 Place the fish roe in a food processor or blender. Place the slice of bread on a plate and sprinkle evenly with enough cold water to dampen the bread. Squeeze the bread in the palm of your hand to remove any excess water then add to the food processor or blender.

2 Roughly chop the potato and add to the food processor or blender with the onion. Process the mixture, on a slow speed if possible. With the motor still running, add the olive oil and lemon juice in a continuous stream, until the mixture is smooth and creamy. Serve chilled, garnished with slices of lemon and chopped fresh parsley.

BELOW
The harbour at Hóra Sfakion is alive with colourful fishing smacks, delivering their catches of squid, sardines, swordfish and prawns.

Classic Greek Salad

HORIATIKI SALATA

❖ ❖ ❖ ❖

The secret of this internationally famous salad is not in its method, but in the ingredients. You need the freshest of everything to create the feeling of lazy days in the Mediterranean sunshine.

Preparation time: about 20 minutes
Cooking time: none
SERVES: 4−6

- *2 large, ripe tomatoes*
- *½ cucumber, diced*
- *1 green pepper, seeded and sliced into rings*
- *50 g/2 oz kalamata olives*
- *1 large red onion, finely sliced*
- *175 g/6 oz feta cheese, cut into 1 cm/½ in cubes*
- *finely grated zest and juice of ½ lemon*
- *50 ml/2 fl oz olive oil*
- *1 tsp dried oregano*
- *coarsely ground salt, to taste*

1 Cut the tomatoes into thin wedges and place in a medium-sized bowl. Add the cucumber, green pepper and olives.

2 Toss the salad together with half of the red onion slices and half of the cubed feta. Scatter the remaining onions and feta over the top of the salad.

3 Sprinkle over the lemon zest and juice, douse with the olive oil and season with the oregano and salt. Gently toss the salad once just before serving.

Greek Potato Salad

PATATOSALATA

◆ ◆ ◆ ◆

Make this salad up to two days before eating it, keep covered in the fridge and forget about it. The flavours will be much stronger when it comes to serving.

Preparation time: about 20 minutes
Cooking time: about 20–25 minutes
SERVES: 4–6

- 900 g/2 lb small new potatoes, scrubbed
- 1 medium red onion, finely sliced into rings
- 50 g/2 oz kalamata olives, washed and
- drained
- 4 tbsp olive oil
- 2 tbsp red wine vinegar
- salt and freshly ground black pepper, to taste
- 1 tsp dried thyme

1 Place the potatoes in a large saucepan and cover with boiling water. Bring back to the boil and cook for 20–25 minutes, or until the potatoes are tender. Drain and allow to cool slightly.

2 Cut the potatoes into 5 mm/¼ in thick slices and arrange in a circular pattern on a serving plate, alternating the potato slices with the onion rings. Scatter over the olives.

3 Combine the oil, vinegar, seasoning and thyme in a screw-top jar and shake well to mix. Pour the dressing over the salad. Cover and chill before serving.

Chickpea Dip
H U M M U S

❖ ❖ ❖ ❖

A classic Meze dish, served with warm pitta bread. There's no need to use dried chickpeas as the canned variety are easier to use and the finished result is just as good.

Preparation time: about 15 minutes
Cooking time: none
SERVES: 4–6

- 400 g/14 oz can chickpeas, washed and drained
- 100 g/4 oz tahini paste
- 50 ml/2 fl oz water
- 2 garlic cloves, crushed
- 50 ml/2 fl oz olive oil
- 85 ml/3 fl oz freshly squeezed lemon juice
- salt and freshly ground black pepper, to taste
- 1 tsp paprika
- chopped fresh parsley to garnish

1 Place the chickpeas in a food processor or blender and purée to a rough texture. Place the tahini paste and water in a medium-sized bowl and mix with a fork until soft and smooth.

2 Add the tahini paste and the garlic to the chickpeas and process until smooth. With the motor still running, add the olive oil and the lemon juice in alternate streams, until the mixture is smooth and creamy. Season to taste with salt and freshly ground black pepper and serve the *hummus* sprinkled with paprika and garnished with chopped fresh parsley.

BELOW
Here, on the south coast near Frangokastello, we can see why Crete is renowned for its beautiful spring wildflowers.

Tuna Fish with Chickpeas
TONOS ME REVITHIA

◆ ◆ ◆ ◆

This wonderful, summery combination of tuna fish and chickpeas makes an excellent cold Meze dish. It's also a quick, easy and nutritious idea for a light lunch.

Preparation time: about 10 minutes
Cooking time: none
SERVES: 4−6

- *400 g/14 oz can chickpeas*
- *2 × 200 g/7 oz cans tuna fish in brine*
- *4 spring onions, finely chopped*
- *1 celery stick, finely chopped*
- *120 ml/4 fl oz olive oil*
- *4 tbsp freshly squeezed lemon juice*
- *finely grated zest of ½ lemon*
- *3 tbsp chopped fresh parsley*
- *1 tbsp chopped fresh dill*
- *salt and freshly ground black pepper, to taste*
- *2 garlic cloves, crushed*
- *¼ tsp mustard powder*
- *fresh parsley and dill, to garnish*

1 Drain the chickpeas and tuna fish and place in a medium-sized bowl. Gently stir in the spring onions and celery.

2 Combine the oil, lemon juice and zest, parsley, dill, salt and pepper, garlic and mustard powder all together in a screw-top jar. Shake well to mix, then pour over the chickpeas and tuna fish. Stir gently to combine, then turn the mixture out on to a serving plate. Cover and chill for several hours before serving, for the best results. Garnish with fresh herbs.

Roast Pepper Salad

PIPERIES OREKTIKO

◆ ◆ ◆ ◆

You can make this salad look especially pretty by using a mixture of coloured peppers.

Preparation time: about 30 minutes
Cooking time: about 20–25 minutes
Oven temperature: 230°C/450°F/Gas 8

SERVES: 4

- 6 peppers of various colours
- 2 onions, finely chopped
- salt and freshly ground black pepper, to taste
- 3 tbsp white wine vinegar
- 50 ml/2 fl oz olive oil
- 3 tbsp chopped fresh parsley, to garnish

1 Preheat the oven to 230°C/450°F/Gas 8. Place the whole peppers on a baking sheet and roast in the oven for 20–25 minutes, or until the peppers have wilted and turned soft.

2 Allow the peppers to cool slightly, then peel away the skins and slice the peppers in half. Scrape out the seeds and cut off the stalks.

3 Slice the pepper flesh into strips and place on a serving plate. Sprinkle the onion, salt and pepper, vinegar and olive oil over the top. Garnish with chopped parsley and chill before serving.

Marinated Meatballs

KEFTEDAKIA ME SALTSA

❖ ❖ ❖ ❖

These mouthwatering, bite-sized morsels are an essential addition to any Meze table. However many you make, they are sure to all be eaten up.

Preparation time: about 15 minutes
plus marinating time
Cooking time: about 55 minutes
Oven temperature: 230°C/450°F/Gas 8/
200°C/400°F/Gas 6
SERVES: 4

- 275 g/10 oz lean minced beef
- 50 g/2 oz fresh white breadcrumbs
- 1 egg, beaten
- 1 tsp made mustard
- 1 tbsp chopped fresh parsley
- pinch of dried oregano
- 1 onion, grated
- salt and finely ground

- black pepper, to taste
- 1 tsp dried mint
- pinch each of ground cinnamon and cloves
- 2 garlic cloves, crushed
- olive oil, for greasing
- 400 g/14 oz can chopped tomatoes
- 50 ml/2 fl oz water
- chopped fresh parsley and mint, to garnish

1 Preheat the oven to 230°C/450°F/Gas 8. Combine all the ingredients, except the canned tomatoes and water, in a large mixing bowl. Mix thoroughly. With slightly damp hands, shape the mixture into 2.5 cm/1 in balls and place on a lightly oiled baking sheet.

2 Bake for 20 minutes, turning each ball over halfway through the cooking time. Drain the meatballs on absorbent kitchen paper, then transfer to a large, shallow ovenproof dish. Set aside.

3 Place the canned tomatoes in a food processor or blender and purée until smooth. Pass through a sieve to remove the seeds and discard. Pour the sieved tomato juice into a small saucepan and add the water. Simmer the sauce for 5 minutes, then pour over the meatballs. Allow to cool, then cover and refrigerate for several hours or overnight.

4 To heat the meatballs through, place in an oven preheated to 200°C/400°F/Gas 6 for about 25–30 minutes, stirring and rearranging once during cooking. Serve garnished with chopped fresh herbs.

Fried Cheese

SAGANAKI

❖ ❖ ❖ ❖

Saganaki is the Greek word for the heavy frying pan or skillet used to cook this dish. Served with a glass of ouzo, this dish is a classic simple Meze.

Preparation time: about 15 minutes
Cooking time: about 10 minutes
SERVES: 4–6

- 225 g/8 oz haloumi cheese
- 50 g/2 oz plain flour
- freshly ground black

- pepper, to taste
- 50 ml/2 fl oz olive oil
- 2 tbsp freshly squeezed lemon juice

1 Cut the cheese into slices 7.5 cm/3 in long and 1 cm/½ in thick. Rinse the slices of cheese under cold running water and pat dry on absorbent kitchen paper.

2 Place the flour on a plate and season with the pepper. Toss the slices of cheese in the flour to coat evenly.

3 Heat the olive oil in a heavy-based frying pan and cook the slices of cheese in batches, shaking off the excess flour before frying. Cook for 2–3 minutes on each side, then transfer to a warm plate and pat with absorbent kitchen paper to soak up any excess oil, if necessary.

4 Sprinkle the *Saganaki* with the lemon juice and serve immediately.

Chicken Filo Rolls

BOUREKAKIA ME KOTA

❖ ❖ ❖

Filo pastry is widely used in Greek cookery and so long as a few simple rules are followed, it is easy to work with and the results are always impressive.

Preparation time: about 35 minutes
Cooking time: about 45 minutes
Oven temperature: 190°C/375°F/Gas 5

SERVES: 8–10

- *450 g/1 lb chicken breast fillets, skinned*
- *1 large onion, quartered*
- *2 celery sticks, roughly chopped*
- *3 peppercorns*
- *pinch of salt*
- *sprig of fresh parsley*
- *50 g/2 oz butter*
- *2 tbsp chopped fresh dill*
- *50 g/2 oz feta cheese, grated*
- *1 egg, beaten*
- *225 g/8 oz filo pastry, thawed if frozen*
- *225 g/8 oz melted butter*

1 Place the chicken fillets in a deep frying pan with the onion, celery, peppercorns, salt and parsley sprigs. Add enough water to cover the chicken and simmer for 20–25 minutes, or until the chicken is cooked through.

2 Remove the chicken from the pan using a slotted spoon and transfer to a food processor or blender with the onion and celery. Discard the cooking liquid and clean the pan ready to use again.

3 Process the chicken and vegetables until the texture is fine. Melt the 50 g/2 oz butter in the cleaned frying pan and sauté the chicken and vegetable mixture for 5–10 minutes, or until lightly browned. Stir in the chopped dill and the grated cheese. Set aside to cool completely, then beat in the egg. Preheat the oven to 190°C/375°F/Gas 5.

4 To make the filo rolls lay the filo pastry out on the work surface and cover with a slightly damp cloth. Separate the first sheet of pastry and lay it on the work surface, keeping the remaining sheets covered to prevent them from drying out. Divide into three equal strips and brush each strip lightly with the melted butter.

5 Place 2 heaped tsp of the chicken mixture at one end of the strip of pastry and fold in the long sides of the strip by about 5 mm/¼ in. Roll up the pastry strip, starting at the filling end, keeping the roll firm and neat. Place the roll on a buttered baking sheet and brush with a little extra melted butter.

6 Repeat the process with the other strips and then continue with another sheet of pastry in the same way. You may need more than one buttered baking sheet.

7 Bake the filo rolls in the oven for about 20 minutes, or until lightly golden and crisp.

Crispy Meat-filled Ovals
COUPES

❖ ❖ ❖ ❖

The crispy coating of the bulgar wheat surrounds a surprise filling of delicately flavoured meat. Another Greek speciality, hard to resist.

Preparation time: about 20 minutes
Cooking time: about 20 minutes

SERVES: 8–10

- *350 g/12 oz bulgar wheat*
- *350 ml/12 fl oz boiling water*
- *salt and freshly ground black pepper, to taste*
- *2 tsp ground cinnamon*
- *1 tbsp vegetable oil, plus*
- *extra for deep frying*
- *175 g/6 oz lean minced pork*
- *4 spring onions, finely chopped*
- *2 tbsp chopped fresh parsley*

1 Place the bulgar wheat in a medium-sized bowl and pour the boiling water over it. Season with salt and freshly ground black pepper and stir in 1 tsp ground cinnamon. Set aside to cool, stirring occasionally.

2 Meanwhile, to make the filling; heat 1 tbsp oil in a frying pan and add the pork and onions. Sauté for about 10–15 minutes, or until the meat is no longer pink and is cooked through. Stir in the parsley and add the remaining ground cinnamon. Season to taste with salt and freshly ground black pepper. Set aside to cool.

3 To shape the *Coupes*; using slightly damp hands, take a small handful of the bulgar mixture and form it into a ball. Using your forefinger and a teaspoon, make a hollow in the centre of the ball and fill it with the pork filling. Pinch the ends of the ball to make an oval and set aside. Continue with the remaining mixture.

4 Heat the oil in a deep-fat fryer and cook the *Coupes* in batches for 3–5 minutes, or until crisp, golden and heated through. Drain the cooked *Coupes* on absorbent kitchen paper and keep warm in a low oven while the other batches cook. Serve warm.

Cheese Filo Triangles

TIROPITTES

◆ ◆ ◆ ◆

A classic Greek Meze dish. Why not double the quantity and freeze half of the *tiropittes* before baking – then you'll have something to fall back on when unexpected guests drop in.

Preparation time: about 25 minutes
Cooking time: about 20 minutes
Oven temperature: 200°C/400°F/Gas 6
SERVES: 8–10

- 225 g/8 oz feta cheese
- 175 g/6 oz cottage cheese
- 2 eggs, beaten
- 2 tbsp chopped fresh parsley
- 1 tbsp chopped fresh mint
- salt and freshly ground black pepper, to taste
- 225 g/8 oz filo pastry, thawed if frozen
- 225 g/8 oz butter, melted

1 Preheat the oven to 200°C/400°F/Gas 6. Place the feta and cottage cheese in a medium-sized bowl and mix well. Beat in the eggs, parsley and mint.

2 To make the *tiropittes* lay the phyllo pastry dough out work surface and cover with a slightly damp cloth. Separate the first sheet of pastry and lay it on the work surface, keeping the remaining sheets covered to prevent them drying out. Divide into three equal strips and brush each strip lightly with the melted butter.

3 Place 2 tsp of the cheese mixture towards the bottom right corner of the pastry strip. Fold that corner diagonally over to the top left corner, to make a small triangle. Then take the bottom left corner and fold it diagonally over to the top right hand corner, and so on, alternately folding the bottom corners in a diagonal pattern to finish up with a firm, neat triangle.

4 Repeat the process with the other strips and then continue with another sheet of pastry in the same way. You may need more than one buttered baking sheet.

5 Bake the *tiropittes* in the oven for 15–20 minutes, or until lightly golden and crisp. Transfer the triangles to a wire rack and serve warm, or allow to cool.

Mini Kebabs

SOUVLAKIA MEZE

✦ ✦ ✦ ✦

Souvlakia is the Greek word for small pieces of meat (and in some cases vegetables too) threaded on to skewers and cooked over a barbecue. This recipe is cooked in the oven, although you could certainly use the barbecue if you wish.

Preparation time: about 15 minutes
Cooking time: about 15–20 minutes
Oven temperature: 190°C/375°F/Gas 5
SERVES: 6–8

- 900 g/2 lb boned leg of lamb
- 120 ml/4 fl oz olive oil
- 1 tsp ground cumin
- 1 tsp dried oregano
- 2 bay leaves, crushed
- 2 garlic cloves, crushed
- 1 onion, very finely chopped
- 50 ml/2 fl oz red wine
- 50 ml/2 fl oz red wine vinegar
- 2 tbsp freshly squeezed lemon juice
- salt and freshly ground black pepper, to taste

1 Cut the lamb into 2.5 cm/1 in cubes and place in a large shallow dish. Combine all the remaining ingredients together in a screw-top jar and shake well.

2 Pour the marinade evenly over the meat and stir to coat. Cover and leave to marinate in a cool place for several hours or overnight.

3 Preheat the oven to 190°C/375°F/Gas 5. Thread the cubes of meat on to skewers and place the kebabs on baking sheets. Bake for 15–20 minutes, turning occasionally, until browned and cooked through. Serve the *Souvlakia* on the skewers with pitta bread and plenty of green salad on the Meze table.

Vegetable Meze

Crispy Fried Courgettes
TEGANITA KOLOKYTHAKIA
◆ ◆ ◆ ◆

Although this recipe uses a batter mixture for coating the courgettes, seasoned flour is also used as a general coating for most vegetables before frying.

Preparation time: about 10 minutes plus chilling time
Cooking time: about 3–5 minutes
SERVES: 4—6

- *350 g/12 oz plain flour*
- *salt and freshly ground black pepper, to taste*
- *pinch of ground cinnamon*
- *175 ml/16 fl oz water*
- *450 g/1 lb courgettes*
- *vegetable oil, for deep frying*

1 Place 225 g/8 oz of the flour in a medium-sized mixing bowl with the seasoning and cinnamon. Make a well in the centre of the flour mixture and pour in the water, mixing simultaneously with a fork, until the batter is thick and smooth and without lumps. Cover the batter and refrigerate for 2–3 hours before using.

2 Trim the courgettes then cut them into 3 mm/⅛ in thick rounds. Dredge the courgette slices in the reserved flour, then toss a few at a time into the batter.

3 Heat the oil and deep-fry the courgettes in batches for 3–5 minutes, or until crisp, golden and cooked through. Remove from the oil with a slotted spoon and drain on absorbent kitchen paper. Keep warm in a low oven while the other batches are cooking. Serve hot.

Meatless Stuffed Vegetables
YEMISTA ORPHANA

◆ ◆ ◆ ◆

This recipe originates from the island of Crete, where the use of rice as the main ingredient for stuffings is most common. The addition of raisins, pine nuts or almonds makes this a truly Cretan creation.

Preparation time: about 1 hour
Cooking time: about 1 hour 30 minutes
Oven temperature: 180°C/350°F/Gas 4

SERVES: 8–10

- 8–10 firm, ripe vegetables, including tomatoes, peppers, courgettes and aubergines
- 85 ml/3 fl oz olive oil
- 6 spring onions, finely chopped
- 225 g/8 oz long-grain rice
- 2 garlic cloves, crushed
- 1 tsp ground cinnamon
- 75 g/3 oz seedless raisins
- 75 g/3 oz toasted pine nuts
- salt and freshly ground black pepper, to taste
- 4 tbsp chopped fresh parsley
- 3 tbsp chopped fresh mint

1 To prepare the vegetables; slice the tops off the tomatoes, peppers, courgettes and aubergines. Scoop out the seeds and flesh from the tomatoes and place in a bowl. Do the same with the aubergines and courgettes, remembering to discard the bitter seeds from the aubergines. Scoop out the seeds from the peppers and discard. Keep each vegetable top intact as they provide the lids for the vegetables when they are stuffed.

2 In a large frying pan, heat 2 tbsp of the olive oil and add the onions. Cook for 3 minutes, then stir in the rice, garlic, cinnamon, raisins, pine nuts and the seeds and pulp reserved from the vegetables. Add enough water to cover the rice and simmer, covered, for 7–10 minutes, or until the rice is tender and the majority of the liquid has been absorbed.

3 Stir the seasoning and herbs into the rice filling and remove from the heat. Preheat the oven to 180°C/350°F/ Gas 4. Stuff the vegetables with the rice filling and place the tops on each vegetable. Arrange the vegetables in a large roasting pan and pour in enough water to just cover the base of the pan.

4 Drizzle over the remaining olive oil and bake for 50–60 minutes, or until the vegetables are tender. Baste the stuffed vegetables several times during cooking, but try not to rearrange them as they may break apart. These *Yemista* can be served warm, but are just as delicious served cold.

Artichoke Heart and Broad Bean Stew
ANGINARES ME KOUKIA
◆ ◆ ◆ ◆

This classic Greek dish requires a little patience in preparing the vegetables and the sauce, but the end result is very much worth the effort.

Preparation time: about 1 hour
Cooking time: about 1 hour 30 minutes
SERVES: 6–8

- *freshly squeezed juice of 3 lemons*
- *600 ml/1 pt water*
- *8 fresh globe artichokes*
- *3 tbsp olive oil*
- *1 large onion, finely chopped*
- *3 garlic cloves, crushed*
- *900 g/2 lb fresh broad beans, podded, washed and drained (or 450 g/ 1 lb frozen broad beans)*

- *100 g/4 oz fennel, thinly sliced*
- *salt and freshly ground black pepper, to taste*
- *½ tsp caster sugar*

FOR THE SAUCE
- *50 ml/2 fl oz olive oil*
- *1 tbsp plain flour*
- *freshly squeezed juice of 1 lemon*
- *salt and freshly ground black pepper, to taste*

1 Place the juice of 2 of the lemons in a large bowl with the water. To prepare the artichokes; using a pair of kitchen scissors, cut off all but 2.5 cm/1 in of the stems and cut away the tough outer leaves. Cut off about 6 cm/2½ in from the top of each artichoke. Open out the leaves of the artichokes and, using a teaspoon, scrape out the hairy chokes and discard. Submerge the prepared artichokes in the lemon water.

2 Heat the olive oil in a large, deep frying pan and sauté the onion and garlic for 3–4 minutes, until the onion has softened. Add the broad beans to the pan and cook for a further 3–4 minutes. Add the artichokes, fennel, salt and freshly ground black pepper, sugar and the remaining lemon juice. Add enough water to the pan to almost cover, then reduce the heat, place the lid on the pan and simmer for 50–60 minutes, or until the vegetables are tender, adding a little extra during cooking if necessary.

3 Using a slotted spoon, transfer the artichokes and beans to a warm serving plate and tent with foil to keep warm. To make the sauce, heat 3 tbsp of olive oil in a medium-sized saucepan and stir in the flour to make a thick paste. Cook the paste for about 1–2 minutes, or until it turns a light golden colour.

4 Whisk in the lemon juice and then the cooking juices from the vegetables into the saucepan. Cook over gentle heat, stirring continuously, until the sauce has thickened and there are no lumps. Season with salt and freshly ground black pepper. Remove the foil tent from the vegetables and pour the sauce over them. Serve warm with plenty of bread to mop up.

Garlic Roast Potatoes
PATATES ME SKORTHO
◆ ◆ ◆ ◆

They taste as good as they sound. Cooked with fresh lemon juice and oregano – once tasted, you'll realize there's no other way to roast potatoes.

Preparation time: about 10 minutes
Cooking time: about 1 hour
Oven temperature: 230°C/450°F/Gas 8
SERVES: 6−8

- 900 g/2 lb large potatoes, peeled
- 50 ml/2 fl oz olive oil
- 120 ml/4 fl oz freshly squeezed lemon juice
- 2 tsp dried oregano
- 3 garlic cloves, very finely chopped
- salt and freshly ground black pepper, to taste
- 120 ml/4 fl oz water

1 Preheat the oven to 230°C/450°F/Gas 8. Cut the potatoes into quarters or eighths lengthways and place in a large, shallow, ovenproof dish.

2 Add the remaining ingredients and stir the potatoes to coat. Bake at the top of the oven, uncovered, for 1 hour, or until lightly golden, crisp on the outside and soft inside. Rearrange the potatoes, and add a little more water if necessary, during cooking.

Spinach Croquettes
KROKETES SPANAKI
◆ ◆ ◆ ◆

In this recipe, rye crispbread crumbs are used to coat the croquettes before frying. If rye crispbread is not available, wholemeal flour is a good substitute.

Preparation time: about 30 minutes
Cooking time: about 20 minutes
SERVES: 6−8

- 25 g/1 oz butter
- 1 onion, very finely chopped
- 900 g/2 lb fresh spinach, roughly chopped
- 175 g/6 oz feta cheese, grated
- 3 eggs, 2 separated
- salt and freshly ground black pepper, to taste
- 75 g/3 oz fresh white breadcrumbs
- 175 g/6 oz rye crispbread crumbs
- olive oil, for shallow frying

1 Melt the butter in a frying pan and add the onion. Sauté for about 3 minutes to soften, then add the spinach. Cook for a further 5 minutes, or until the spinach is softened, then remove from the heat.

2 Transfer the spinach mixture to a medium-sized mixing bowl and stir in the cheese, whole egg and the egg yolks. Season with salt and freshly ground black pepper and stir in the fresh breadcrumbs.

3 Place the crispbread crumbs on one plate and the egg whites on another. Using slightly damp hands, shape the mixture into small croquettes. Roll the croquettes in the crispbread to coat, then in the egg white, and finally in the crispbread again. Repeat this procedure with the remaining croquettes.

4 Heat the oil in a frying pan and shallow-fry the croquettes in batches for about 5–8 minutes, or until golden brown and cooked through, turning and rearranging them frequently during cooking. Using a slotted spoon, transfer the croquettes to a dish lined with absorbent kitchen paper to drain. Keep warm in a low oven while the remainder are being cooked. Serve warm or cold.

Cauliflower Baked with Tomatoes and Feta
KOUNOUPITHI KAPAMA

◆ ◆ ◆ ◆

This dish is enlivened with a strong flavour of tomatoes combined with the typically Greek use of ground cinnamon to give that extra special taste.

Preparation time: about 30 minutes
Cooking time: about 1 hour 30 minutes
Oven temperature: 190°C/375°F/Gas 5
SERVES: 4–6

- *85 ml/3 fl oz olive oil*
- *1 onion, sliced*
- *2 garlic cloves, crushed*
- *8 tomatoes, seeded and chopped*
- *large pinch of ground cinnamon*
- *2 tsp dried oregano*
- *salt and freshly ground black pepper, to taste*
- *1 large cauliflower, cut into florets*
- *1 tbsp freshly squeezed lemon juice*
- *75 g/3 oz feta cheese, grated*

1 Heat 2–3 tbsp olive oil in a heavy-based frying pan and sauté the onion and garlic for 3–4 minutes, or until the onion has softened.

2 Add the chopped tomatoes, cinnamon and oregano and season with salt and pepper. Stir and simmer, covered, for 5 minutes.

3 Preheat the oven to 190°C/375°F/Gas 5. Add the cauliflower to the tomato mixture, cover, and simmer for a further 10–15 minutes or until the cauliflower is just tender. Remove from the heat.

4 Transfer the cauliflower and tomato mixture to a large, shallow dish and drizzle over the remaining olive oil. Sprinkle over the lemon juice and grated feta. Bake for 45–50 minutes, or until the cauliflower is soft and the cheese has melted. Serve warm.

Easter Menu

Crispy Meat-Filled Ovals
Coupes

◆

Easter Lamb Soup
Mageiritsa

◆

Spicy Lamb Stew with Mint and Sage
Arni me Diosmo kai Fascomilo

◆

Lamb Kebabs
Souvlakia

◆

Garlic Roast Potatoes
Patates me Skortho

◆

Green Bean Ragout
Fassolakia Yiahni

◆

Easter Bread
Tsoureki

◆

Sweet Cheese Pastries
Kaltsounia Cretis

◆

Easter Biscuits
Koulourakia Lambriatika

◆

**Wine: Naoussa Grande Reserve
(Full-bodied red)**

◆

Stuffed Vine Leaves

DOLMADES

◆ ◆ ◆ ◆

Use fresh vine leaves if they are available. Choose young, tender leaves of a good size. Wash and drain them well, then trim the tough stems with scissors. Boil the leaves in salted water for about 15 minutes, then drain and rinse under cold running water.

Preparation time: about 45 minutes
Cooking time: about 2 hours 30 minutes
SERVES: 10—12

- *30 vine leaves in brine, rinsed well*
- *50 ml/2 fl oz olive oil*
- *1 large onion, very finely chopped*
- *100 g/4 oz long-grain rice*
- *2 garlic cloves, crushed*
- *50 g/2 oz pine nuts*
- *50 g/2 oz raisins*
- *1 tsp ground cumin*
- *600 ml/1 pt plus 3 tbsp water*
- *4 tbsp chopped fresh dill*
- *4 tbsp chopped fresh parsley*
- *2 tbsp chopped fresh mint*
- *salt and freshly ground black pepper, to taste*
- *1 egg, beaten*
- *juice of 1 lemon*

1 Fill a large saucepan with water and bring to a rolling boil. Drop the vine leaves into the water and cook for 3–5 minutes, or until softened. Drain well and set aside.

2 Heat 2 tbsp olive oil in a large frying pan and sauté the onion for 3–5 minutes, or until softened. Add the rice and cook for a further 3–5 minutes, or until lightly coloured, stirring continuously with a wooden spoon.

3 Add the garlic, pine nuts, raisins and cumin and stir in 300 ml/½ pt water. Cover and simmer for about 10 minutes, or until the rice is tender and the liquid has been absorbed. Remove from the heat and set aside to cool down.

4 Stir the chopped fresh herbs into the rice mixture and season with salt and freshly ground black pepper. Stir in 1 tbsp of the remaining olive oil and the beaten egg.

5 Place the remaining olive oil in a large saucepan with 3 tbsp water. Line the base of the saucepan with 3–4 vine leaves. (You can use any that are torn or otherwise imperfect for this.) To stuff the remaining vine leaves; place about 1 tsp of the rice mixture in the centre of each leaf and neatly fold the leaf around the filling to encase it completely.

6 Place the stuffed vine leaf in the base of the saucepan, seam-side down, and repeat with the remaining vine leaves, layering them on top of each other neatly. Sprinkle over the lemon juice and about 300 ml/½ pt of water. Place a plate, upside-down, on top of the dolmades to keep them in position during cooking. Cover with a lid and simmer for about 2 hours, or until the vine leaves are tender and the rice is cooked through. Serve warm or cold.

BELOW
Mountainous Mykonos affords beautiful views of the island of *Delos where, in Greek mythology, Apollo and Artemis were born.*

Green Bean Ragout

FASSOLAKIA YIAHNI

❖ ❖ ❖ ❖

In Greece, fresh green beans can be found in several different varieties, all of which are suitable for this recipe. Greeks usually eat this dish cold, but it can be served warm too.

Preparation time: about 15 minutes
Cooking time: about 2 hours
SERVES: 6–8

- 50 ml/2 fl oz olive oil
- 2 onions, chopped
- 700 g/1½ lb fresh green beans, topped and tailed
- 3 medium potatoes, peeled and quartered
- 2 garlic cloves, crushed
- 4 ripe tomatoes, skinned,
- seeded and roughly chopped
- 50 ml/2 fl oz water
- salt and freshly ground black pepper, to taste
- 75 g/3 oz feta cheese, grated

1 Heat the oil in a large saucepan and add the onions. Cook for 3–4 minutes, or until softened but not browned. Add the green beans and the potatoes and stir to coat in olive oil. Add the garlic and cook for a further 5 minutes.

2 Add the tomatoes and the water. Season with salt and freshly ground black pepper and reduce the heat and simmer, covered, for about 1½ hours, or until the beans and potatoes are soft, adding a little extra water if necessary. Sprinkle the grated feta cheese over the top, if serving warm.

FACING PAGE
Why not enjoy a glass of retsina at this pretty taverna on the curve of Réthimnon harbour?

Spinach Pie
S P A N A K O P I T T A

◆ ◆ ◆ ◆

Pites – Greek for savoury pies – are a welcome treat at any table, filled with spinach, cheese, courgettes or meat, cut into slices or wedges and served as simple fare at informal occasions.

Preparation time: about 45 minutes
Cooking time: about 1 hour
Oven temperature: 190°C/375°F/Gas 5
S E R V E S : 8 – 1 0

- *6 sheets filo pastry, thawed if frozen*
- *100 g/4 oz butter, melted*
- *85 ml/3 fl oz olive oil*
- *1 bunch of spring onions, trimmed and chopped*
- *1 leek, trimmed and chopped*
- *700 g/1½ lb fresh spinach, chopped*
- *6 tbsp chopped fresh dill*
- *4 tbsp chopped fresh*
- *parsley*
- *1 egg, beaten*
- *350 g/12 oz feta cheese, crumbled*
- *2 tbsp kefalotyri or fresh parmesan cheese, grated*
- *½ tsp grated nutmeg*
- *½ tsp ground cumin*
- *salt and freshly ground black pepper, to taste*
- *1 egg yolk mixed with 2 tbsp milk, to glaze*

1 Lay one sheet of filo pastry out on the work surface, keeping the remainder covered with a slightly damp cloth. Brush the single sheet evenly with the melted butter, then place another sheet of filo pastry on top. Brush again with the melted butter and repeat with a final sheet. Brush with melted butter. Use to line a buttered 26 cm/10½ in pie dish.

2 Preheat the oven to 190°C/375°F/Gas 5. To make the pie filling; heat 2 tbsp of the olive oil in a large frying pan and sauté the spring onions and leek for about 5 minutes or until softened. Add the spinach and cook for a further 5–7 minutes, or until wilted. Strain the spinach mixture in a sieve to remove the excess liquid. Set aside to cool.

3 In a large bowl, combine the spinach mixture with the herbs, beaten egg, cheeses, spices and seasoning. Mix well. Spread the spinach mixture evenly over the base of the lined pie dish. Repeat the layering of buttered filo pastry with the remaining sheets, then use to top the pie. Press the edges of the pastry together firmly to seal and cut away the excess pastry.

4 Make a small incision in the centre of the pie, then brush the top with the beaten yolk and milk mixture, to glaze. Bake for about 40–45 minutes, or until the pastry is crisp and golden. Allow to cool slightly in the dish before cutting into slices to serve warm – it is also delicious served cold.

Rolled Cabbage Leaves

LAHANODOLMADES

❖ ❖ ❖ ❖

Cabbage leaves are a favourite amongst the Greeks for stuffing. The fillings can vary from meat to rice mixtures, but they are always served hot and often with Greek yoghurt or soured cream.

Preparation time: about 45 minutes
Cooking time: about 3 hours
SERVES: 6−8

- *1 savoy cabbage*
- *freshly squeezed juice of 1 lemon*

FOR THE FILLING
- *6 tbsp olive oil*
- *1 large onion, finely chopped*
- *100 g/4 oz long-grain rice*
- *100 g/4 oz lean minced*

- *beef or lamb*
- *2 garlic cloves, crushed*
- *3 tbsp chopped fresh dill*
- *2 tbsp chopped fresh parsley*
- *1 tsp ground cumin*
- *1 tsp dried mint*
- *salt and freshly ground black pepper, to taste*
- *150 ml/¼ pt water*

1 Using a sharp vegetable knife, cut the core out of the cabbage and carefully separate the leaves, without ripping them, if possible. Wash and drain the leaves, place them in a large saucepan of boiling water and cook for 2–3 minutes to soften slightly. Drain and rinse under cold running water. Set aside.

2 To prepare the filling; heat 2 tbsp of the olive oil in a large frying pan and sauté the onion for about 3 minutes, or until softened. Stir in the rice and cook for a further 2 minutes, then add the minced meat. Cook for about 5 minutes, stirring the meat until it is no longer pink. Add the garlic, herbs and spices and season with salt and freshly ground black pepper. Add the water to the meat mixture, cover and simmer for 15–20 minutes, or until the meat is almost cooked and the rice has softened, adding a little extra water if necessary.

3 Place another 2 tbsp of the olive oil in the base of a large saucepan. Line the base of the saucepan with 3–4 cabbage leaves. (You can use any that are torn or otherwise imperfect for this.) To stuff the remaining cabbage leaves, place about 2 tsp of the filling towards the bottom centre of the leaf. Fold both sides of the leaf over to encase the filling, then roll up, starting from the bottom. Carefully place the rolled leaf, seam-side down, in the base of the saucepan. Repeat with the remaining cabbage leaves, layering the rolls on top of each other.

4 Add enough water to come about 4 cm/1½ in up the sides of the rolled leaves. Add the remaining olive oil and the lemon juice. Place a plate upsidedown on top of the stuffed cabbage leaves to keep them in position during cooking. Cover with a lid and simmer for 2–2½ hours, or until the leaves are almost translucent and the filling is cooked through, adding a little extra water during cooking, if necessary.

FACING PAGE
A Mykonos windmill in early autumn . . . this Aegean island has a church for every day of the year.

Moussaka with Aubergines
MOUSSAKA ME MELITZANES

❖ ❖ ❖

This is a meatless version of the classic Greek dish. Rice, feta, currants and seeds make a delicious and wholesome alternative filling.

Preparation time: about 30 minutes plus soaking
Cooking time: about 1 hour 30 minutes
Oven temperature: 190°C/375°F/Gas 5
SERVES: 10–12

- 3–4 *aubergines*
- *salt*
- *olive oil, for shallow frying*
- 150 g/5 oz short-grain brown rice
- 450 g/1 lb can chopped tomatoes
- 1 onion, chopped
- 3 tbsp chopped fresh parsley
- 120 ml/4 fl oz olive oil
- 3 garlic cloves, chopped
- freshly ground black pepper, to taste
- 2 tbsp sunflower seeds

- 25 g/1 oz pine nuts
- 75 g/3 oz currants
- 100 g/4 oz feta cheese, grated

FOR THE SAUCE
- 175 g/6 oz plain flour
- 100 g/4 oz butter
- 900 ml/1½ pt warm milk
- 5 eggs plus 1 egg yolk
- salt and freshly ground black pepper, to taste
- 350 g/12 oz kefalotyri or feta cheese, grated

1 Cut the aubergines lengthways into thin slices and place them in a shallow dish. Cover with cold water and dredge with plenty of salt. Soak for 30 minutes. Rinse the aubergine slices under cold running water and pat dry on absorbent kitchen paper. Heat the olive oil for shallow frying and fry the sliced aubergines, in batches if necessary, for 10–15 minutes, or until golden and soft, turning them over during cooking. Using a slotted spoon, transfer to a dish lined with absorbent kitchen paper to drain. Set aside.

2 Wash and drain the rice. Cook in boiling water for 20–25 minutes or until tender. Drain and return to the pan with the tomatoes, onion, parsley, olive oil and garlic and season with salt and freshly ground black pepper. Simmer, stirring occasionally, for about 10 minutes or until the liquid has been absorbed. Remove from the heat and stir in the seeds, nuts, currants and cheese. Set aside.

3 Preheat the oven to 190°C/375°F/Gas 5. To make the sauce; place the flour and butter in a large saucepan and heat gently, stirring continuously, until the butter has melted and the mixture forms a smooth paste. Gradually stir in the warm milk, making sure there are no lumps. Bring the sauce to the boil, stirring continuously until thickened. Remove from the heat and beat in the eggs, yolk, salt and freshly ground black pepper and the cheese.

4 Place half the fried aubergines in a layer on the bottom of a 25 × 30 cm/10 × 12 in shallow ovenproof dish. Add the rice mixture and spread evenly, then add the remaining aubergine slices. Top with the thick cheese sauce and bake the moussaka in the oven for 35–40 minutes, or until the surface is golden and the dish is heated through. Allow to cool slightly, then cut into portions and serve.

Greek Meze Mushrooms

MANITARIA

◆ ◆ ◆ ◆

This Meze dish is best kept simple, with the use of fresh, firm mushrooms and a good-quality olive oil for the best flavour.

Preparation time: about 10 minutes
Cooking time: about 15 minutes
SERVES: 6–8

- 150 ml/¼ pt olive oil
- 120 ml/4 fl oz dry white wine
- salt and freshly ground black pepper, to taste
- 1 tsp dried thyme
- 3 garlic cloves, crushed
- 4 tbsp chopped fresh parsley
- 550 g/1¼ lb tiny button mushrooms, cleaned
- freshly squeezed juice of 1 lemon
- chopped fresh parsley, to garnish

1 Place all the ingredients, except the mushrooms and half the lemon juice, in a large saucepan and bring to the boil. Reduce the heat and stir in the mushrooms. Cover and simmer for 8–10 minutes.

2 Transfer the mushrooms and the liquid to a serving dish and allow to cool completely. Serve at room temperature, sprinkled with the remaining lemon juice and garnished with chopped fresh parsley.

BELOW
Bars and tavernas, leather shops and stalls jostle for custom along Haniá's harbour promenade. In spring, out of main season, the pace is more leisurely.

Aubergine Ragout
MELITZANES YIAHNI

◆ ◆ ◆ ◆

This richly flavoured dish should be accompanied at the Meze table by plenty of fresh bread, feta cheese and a full-bodied red wine to wash it down.

Preparation time: about 20 minutes plus standing time
Cooking time: about 50–60 minutes
SERVES: 4–6

- *3 large aubergines*
- *salt*
- *120 ml/4 fl oz olive oil*
- *2 onions, halved and sliced*
- *4 garlic cloves, crushed*
- *700 g/1½ lb tomatoes,*
- *skinned, seeded and chopped*
- *3 tbsp chopped fresh parsley*
- *salt and freshly ground black pepper, to taste*

1 Cut the aubergines into 5 cm/2 in thick chunks and place in a colander. Generously sprinkle with salt and set aside for 30–45 minutes. Rinse the aubergines under cold running water and drain well.

2 Heat the olive oil in a large saucepan and add the onion. Cook for 3–5 minutes, or until the onion has softened, then add the aubergine chunks. Stir to coat in the oil.

3 Add the garlic, tomatoes and parsley to the saucepan and season with salt and freshly ground black pepper. Add a little water to moisten the mixture, if necessary, then cover and simmer for about 50–55 minutes, or until the aubergines are very soft and the sauce has thickened. Serve warm or cold.

Baked Mixed Vegetables

B R I A M

◆ ◆ ◆ ◆

This light and easy-to-prepare dish is a favourite throughout Greece during spring and summer.

Preparation time: about 10 minutes
Cooking time: about 2 hours
Oven temperature: 180°C/350°F/Gas 4
SERVES: 6–8

- 85 ml/3 fl oz olive oil
- 3 onions, sliced
- 700 g/1½ lb small potatoes, peeled and halved or sliced into thick rounds
- 700 g/1½ lb courgettes, cut into 1 cm/½ in chunks
- 8 ripe tomatoes, skinned and roughly chopped
- 2 peppers, seeded and sliced into rings
- 4 garlic cloves, finely chopped
- 1 tsp dried oregano
- 4 tbsp chopped fresh parsley
- 2 tbsp chopped fresh dill
- salt and freshly ground black pepper, to taste
- 120 ml/4 fl oz water

1 Preheat the oven to 180°C/350°F/Gas 4. Heat 2 tbsp of the olive oil in a frying pan and sauté the onion for 3–5 minutes, until softened but not coloured. Remove from the heat.

2 Combine the sautéed onion with the prepared potatoes, courgettes, tomatoes, peppers, garlic, herbs and seasoning in a large roasting pan. Add the water and bake for 1½–2 hours, until the vegetables are tender and cooked through, rearranging them twice during cooking. Serve warm or cold.

47

Black-Eye Beans with Greens
LOUVIA ME LAHANA

 ◆ ◆ ◆ ◆

A typical Greek dish served in springtime, when the winter rains have gone and the leafy greens are at their best. Chard leaves are best to use in this recipe, but spinach makes a good substitute.

Preparation time: about 30 minutes
Cooking time: about 30 minutes
SERVES: 4—6

- 225 g/8 oz black-eye beans, soaked overnight
- 450 g/1 lb chard or spinach leaves
- olive oil, to drizzle
- 2 tbsp freshly squeezed
- lemon juice
- salt and freshly ground black pepper, to taste
- chopped fresh parsley, to garnish

1 Place the beans in a medium-sized saucepan and cover with water. Bring to the boil, then drain and rinse the beans.

2 Return the beans to the saucepan and cover with fresh water. Bring to the boil again and simmer for 25–30 minutes, or until the beans are almost tender, adding a little extra water during cooking if necessary to keep the beans covered.

3 Shred the greens and stir into the beans and cook for a further 3–4 minutes, or until the greens have softened. Drain well and turn into a serving dish. Drizzle over the olive oil and lemon juice. Season with salt and freshly ground black pepper and serve warm, garnished with chopped fresh parsley.

LEFT
The weaving of Palm Sunday crosses is a traditional Eastertide craft in Greece.

Meat Meze

Meatballs in Tomato Sauce

◆

Moussaka

◆

Chunks of Lamb in Filo Pastry

Baked Pasta Casserole

Meat and Rice Balls in Lemon Sauce

Pork and Wheat

Greek Hamburgers

Spicy Lamb Stew with Mint and Sage

Sausage and Pepper Stew

Stewed Steak

Beef and Onion Stew

Lamb Chops with Cheese

◆

Lamb Kebabs

◆

Fresh Ham Macaroni

◆

Lamb Cooked in Foil

◆

Minced Meat Kebabs

Meatballs in Tomato Sauce

GIOUVARLAKIA

This rich, tasty dish can be made well in advance and kept in the fridge – in fact, it tastes better reheated the next day.

Preparation time: about 30 minutes
Cooking time: about 30 minutes
SERVES: 6–8

- 700 g/1½ lb minced lamb
- 2 slices brown bread
- 4 tbsp milk
- 1 tbsp olive oil
- 1 onion, chopped
- 1 tomato, skinned, seeded and chopped
- 100 g/4 oz long-grain rice
- 1 tbsp chopped fresh mint
- pinch of ground cinnamon
- 2 tbsp chopped fresh parsley
- 1 egg, beaten
- 50 ml/2 fl oz red wine
- salt and freshly ground black pepper, to taste
- 1.2 ml/2 pt water
- 4 tbsp tomato purée
- 1 garlic clove, crushed
- chopped fresh parsley, to garnish

1 Place the minced lamb in a large mixing bowl. Remove the crusts from the bread and place the bread on a plate. Sprinkle over the milk and allow to soak for 10 minutes, or until all the milk has been soaked up into the bread. Add the bread to the mixing bowl. Using your hand, mix the meat and bread together thoroughly.

2 Heat the olive oil in a small saucepan and sauté the onion and chopped tomato flesh for about 5 minutes. Add to the mixing bowl with the rice, mint, cinnamon, parsley, beaten egg, wine and salt and freshly ground black pepper. Mix well to combine all the ingredients.

3 Place the water in a large, deep frying pan and stir in the tomato purée. Add the garlic and heat gently to bring to the boil. Simmer for 5 minutes.

4 Using slightly damp hands, shape the meat mixture into round balls, about the size of a golf ball, and carefully place them in the simmering tomato sauce. Cover the frying pan and cook for about 30 minutes, or until the rice is cooked and the sauce has thickened. Serve garnished with chopped parsley.

Moussaka

◆ ◆ ◆ ◆

Recognized as the national dish of Greece – sliced aubergines layered with onions and minced lamb, then topped with bechamel sauce.

Preparation time: about 1 hour
Cooking time: about 2 hours and 30 minutes
Oven temperature: 180°C/350°F/Gas 4

SERVES: 10–12

- *5 large aubergines, trimmed and sliced lengthways*
- *salt*
- *olive oil, for brushing*
- *100 g/4 oz fresh white breadcrumbs*
- *175 g/6 oz feta cheese, grated*

FOR THE BECHAMEL SAUCE
- *100 g/4 oz butter*
- *100 g/4 oz plain flour*
- *1.2 l/2 pt warm milk*
- *salt and freshly ground black pepper, to taste*
- *large pinch ground nutmeg*
- *3 egg yolks*

FOR THE MEAT SAUCE
- *2 tbsp olive oil*
- *4 onions, roughly chopped*
- *1.1 kg/2½ lb lean minced lamb*
- *2 × 400 g/14 oz cans chopped tomatoes*
- *3 garlic cloves, crushed*
- *½ tsp ground cinnamon*
- *pinch of ground allspice*
- *salt and freshly ground black pepper, to taste*
- *4 tbsp tomato purée*
- *120 ml/4 fl oz dry red wine*

1 Lay the slices of aubergine out on the work surface and sprinkle evenly with salt on both sides. Allow to "sweat" for 30 minutes, then rinse the slices thoroughly under cold running water.

2 Lay as many slices of aubergine as possible on the rack of a grill pan and brush generously with olive oil. Grill for 5–10 minutes, turning the slices over and brushing again with olive oil, until they are golden brown on both sides. Set aside and repeat with the remaining slices of aubergine.

3 Grease a 28 × 38 × 7.5 cm/11 × 15 × 3 in ovenproof dish with olive oil and sprinkle evenly with the breadcrumbs. To make the bechamel sauce; melt the butter in a large saucepan and stir in the flour to make a thick paste. Cook the paste for 30 seconds, then remove from the heat. Gradually add the milk, stirring after each addition to prevent lumps from forming. Return the sauce to the heat and gradually bring to the boil, stirring continuously, until thick and bubbling. Remove from the heat and season with salt and freshly ground black pepper and the nutmeg. Cool the sauce slightly, then beat in the egg yolks. Cover the surface of the sauce with a piece of greaseproof paper to prevent a skin from forming and set aside.

4 To make the meat sauce; heat the olive oil in a large, heavy saucepan and sauté the onion until softened. Add the minced lamb and stir. Cook, stirring frequently, for about 10 minutes, or until the meat is no longer pink. Add the tomatoes, garlic and spices and season with salt and freshly ground black pepper. Stir in the tomato purée and the red wine.

5 Reduce the heat, cover, and simmer the sauce for about 45 minutes, adding a little water if necessary. Remove the cover for the last 15 minutes of the cooking time to allow all of the moisture to evaporate. Set the sauce aside to cool slightly.

6 Preheat the oven to 180°C/350°F/Gas 4. Arrange a layer of sliced aubergines in the bottom of the prepared dish and cover with a layer of the meat sauce. Add another layer of the aubergine slices and another of the meat sauce. Continue layering in this fashion, finishing with a layer of sliced aubergine. Carefully pour the bechamel sauce on top of the dish and spread evenly. Sprinkle with the grated feta cheese and bake in the oven for about 1 hour, or until the top is golden brown and the Moussaka is heated through. Serve warm.

BELOW
A quintessentially Greek vista on the Lasithi Plateau.

Chunks of Lamb in Filo Pastry
ARNI EXOHIKO

❖ ❖ ❖ ❖

Exohiko is the Greek word for countryside and, as the name suggests, this dish would be perfect for a Meze picnic. Easily made in advance, this dish can also be frozen unbaked, then thawed and finished off in the oven when required.

Preparation time: about 1 hour
Cooking time: about 3 hours
Oven temperature: 190°C/375°F/Gas 5
SERVES: 10–15

- 3.6 kg/8 lb leg of lamb
- 4 garlic cloves, cut into slivers
- salt and freshly ground black pepper, to taste
- 2 tsp dried oregano
- 350 g/12 oz butter, melted
- 3 tbsp freshly squeezed lemon juice

- 2 carrots, peeled
- 2 celery sticks, trimmed
- 1 onion, quartered
- 450 g/1 lb filo pastry, thawed if frozen
- 450 g/1 lb fresh white breadcrumbs
- 225 g/8 oz feta cheese, grated

BELOW
Delicate wrought-iron tracery is a common feature of Hellenic architecture.

1 Preheat the oven to 190°C/375°F/Gas 5. Using a sharp knife, make small incisions all over the lamb and insert the slivers of garlic into them. Place the lamb in a roasting tin. Season with salt and freshly ground black pepper and sprinkle over the oregano. Drizzle over a little of the melted butter and pour over the lemon juice. Add the carrot, celery and onion to the pan and roast the lamb for 2–2½ hours, until the meat is tender and the juices run clear. Transfer the joint to a chopping board and cut the meat into 2.5 cm/1 in chunks, discarding the fat and bone. Allow the chunks of meat to cool.

2 Take one sheet of the filo pastry, keeping the remainder covered with a slightly damp cloth, and brush lightly with melted butter. Fold the sheet in half. Brush once again with melted butter, then sprinkle over a few of the breadcrumbs.

3 Place a few chunks of meat towards one end of the pastry and sprinkle over a little of the cheese. Fold up the pastry around the filling, enclosing it securely, and place seam-side down on a lightly oiled baking sheet. Repeat with the remaining filo pastry and filling. Brush the parcels with the remaining melted butter and bake for about 30 minutes, or until the pastry has turned crisp and golden.

Baked Pasta Casserole

PASTITSIO

◆ ◆ ◆ ◆

The name of this dish is undoubtedly of Italian origin, although the method of cooking pasta with meat in a casserole is undoubtably Greek.

*Preparation time: about 1 hour
Cooking time: about 2 hours
Oven temperature: 180°C/350°F/Gas 4*
SERVES: 10–12

- 6 tbsp olive oil
- 3 onions, chopped
- 700 g/1½ lb lean minced beef
- 2 garlic cloves, crushed
- 2 × 400 g/14 oz cans chopped tomatoes
- 2 tsp ground cinnamon
- 1 tsp ground nutmeg
- 1½ tsp ground allspice
- salt and freshly ground black pepper, to taste

- 700 g/1½ lb spaghetti

FOR THE CHEESE SAUCE
- 100 g/4 oz butter
- 100 g/4 oz plain flour
- 1.2 l/2 pt warm milk
- salt and freshly ground black pepper, to taste
- 225 g/8 oz feta or kefalotyri cheese, grated
- 3 egg yolks

1 Heat 2 tbsp of the olive oil in a large saucepan and add the onions. Sauté until softened but not coloured. Add the minced beef to the saucepan and cook, stirring frequently, until the meat is no longer pink.

2 Add the garlic, chopped tomatoes and spices, and season with salt and freshly ground black pepper. Cover and simmer for about 40 minutes, adding a little water if necessary during cooking. Remove the cover for the last 10 minutes of cooking time to allow the remaining moisture to evaporate. Cool slightly.

3 Meanwhile, bring a large saucepan of water to the boil and drop in the spaghetti. Boil for about 10–15 minutes – the pasta should be cooked until just tender. Drain and rinse under hot running water. Return the spaghetti to the saucepan and stir in another 2 tbsp of the olive oil.

4 To make the cheese sauce; melt the butter in a large saucepan and stir in the flour to make a thick paste. Cook the paste for 30 seconds, then remove from the heat. Gradually add the warm milk, stirring well after each addition to prevent any lumps from forming. Return the sauce to the heat and season with salt and freshly ground black pepper. Stir in the grated cheese and gradually bring to the boil, stirring continuously, until the sauce has thickened and is bubbling. Beat in the egg yolks thoroughly.

5 Preheat the oven to 180°C/350°F/Gas 4. Grease a 28 × 38 × 7.5 cm/11 × 15 × 3 in ovenproof dish with the remaining olive oil and place half the spaghetti in the base of the dish. Add the meat sauce, spreading it evenly over the pasta, then top with the remaining spaghetti. Pour the cheese sauce evenly over the top of the dish and bake for about 45 minutes, or until the top is golden brown and the *Pastitsio* is cooked through.

Meat and Rice Balls in Lemon Sauce

YUVERLAKIA

Yuverlakia **means 'little spheres'; this dish is a cross between a hearty soup and stew.**

Preparation time: about 30 minutes
Cooking time: about 50 minutes

SERVES: 8–10

- 450 g/1 lb minced pork
- 150 g/5 oz long-grain rice
- 1 large onion, finely chopped
- 2 garlic cloves, crushed
- 4 tbsp very finely chopped fresh parsley
- 2 tbsp chopped fresh mint
- 1 tsp dried oregano
- 1 egg yolk

- salt and freshly ground black pepper, to taste
- flour, for dredging
- 3 tbsp olive oil
- 3 eggs, beaten
- freshly squeezed juice of 2 lemons, strained
- chopped fresh parsley, to garnish

1 Combine the minced pork, rice, onion, garlic and herbs in a large mixing bowl. Add the egg yolk and season with salt and freshly ground black pepper. Mix thoroughly to combine all the ingredients. Using slightly damp hands, shape the mixture into 5 cm/2 in balls and dredge with flour.

2 Place the olive oil in a large, deep frying pan with the meatballs. Add enough boiling water to just cover the meatballs. Cover and simmer for 35–40 minutes, or until the meat and rice are cooked, adding a little extra water to keep the meatballs covered during cooking if necessary.

3 To make the lemon sauce; beat together the eggs and lemon juice until frothy. Whisk in 2 tbsp of the cooking liquid from the meatballs, whisking vigorously to prevent curdling. Remove the frying pan from the heat and pour the egg mixture over the meatballs. Return the frying pan to the heat and stir continuously, until thickened. Do not allow the sauce to boil. Transfer the meatballs and sauce to a warm serving dish and garnish with chopped fresh parsley.

Pork and Wheat

KISKEKI

This ancient and simple dish from rural Greece would have made use of the 'gleena' or lard from the pig when made in days gone by. Olive oil is used here as a healthier and more readily available substitute. Whole wheat is available from most health food shops.

Preparation time: about 30 minutes
Cooking time: about 4 hours
SERVES: 8 — 10

- *50 ml/2 fl oz olive oil*
- *900 g/2 lb lean pork fillet, cut into large pieces*
- *salt and freshly ground black pepper, to taste*
- *2–3 red chillies, seeded and finely chopped*
- *225 g/8 oz whole wheat*
- *50 g/2 oz butter*
- *2 onions, peeled and chopped*
- *1 tsp ground cumin*
- *Greek yoghurt, to serve*

1 Heat the oil in a large saucepan and add the pork, turning, to brown evenly. Add enough water to cover the meat and slowly bring to the boil. Season with salt and freshly ground black pepper, add the chopped chillies, reduce the heat and simmer, covered, for about 2 hours, or until the meat is extremely tender.

2 Meanwhile, place the whole wheat in a medium-sized saucepan with enough water to cover it by 7.5 cm/3 in. Bring to the boil, stir and reduce the heat. Simmer, covered, for about 1½ hours, or until the wheat is tender. Remove from the heat and drain.

3 Melt the butter in a frying pan and sauté the onions until softened but not coloured. Set aside. Transfer the cooked pork to a chopping board. Using two forks, shred the meat into small pieces and place on a warm serving dish with the wheat. Stir to combine and pour over the sautéed onion and butter. Sprinkle over the cumin and serve with Greek yoghurt.

Greek Hamburgers

KEPHTEDES

◆ ◆ ◆ ◆

Greek hamburgers can be served hot or cold, but they should never be overcooked.

Preparation time: about 30 minutes
Cooking time: about 40 minutes
SERVES: 6—8

- 450 g/1 lb minced beef
- 2 slices of bread, crusts removed
- 2 tbsp milk
- 3 tbsp olive oil
- 50 g/2 oz butter
- 1 small onion, finely chopped
- 1 garlic clove, crushed
- 1 small carrot, finely

- grated
- 1 tomato, skinned and chopped
- 4 tbsp chopped fresh parsley
- 2 tbsp red wine
- salt and freshly ground black pepper, to taste
- 225 g/8 oz plain flour

1 Place the minced beef in a large mixing bowl. Place the bread on a plate and sprinkle over the milk. Allow to soak for 5 minutes, or until the milk has been absorbed, then add to the minced beef. Mix well to combine. Set aside for the time being.

2 Heat 1 tbsp of the olive oil and 15 g/½ oz of the butter in a frying pan until the butter has melted. Add the onion, garlic, carrot and tomato and sauté for about 7 minutes, or until the onion has browned.

3 Add the sautéed vegetables to the mixing bowl with the parsley, wine and salt and freshly ground black pepper. Mix thoroughly. Set aside for about 30 minutes.

4 Sprinkle the flour evenly over a baking sheet. Using slightly damp hands, shape the meat mixture into burger shapes, then drop into the flour and coat on both sides. Place the coated burgers on a clean baking sheet, lined with greaseproof paper.

5 Heat the remaining olive oil and butter in a large frying pan until sizzling. Fry the burgers in batches, cooking for about 5 minutes on each side, taking care when turning them over. Add a little extra olive oil and butter as you cook the batches if necessary. Transfer the cooked burgers to a warm serving plate while you cook the remaining burgers. Serve warm or cold.

Spicy Lamb Stew with Mint and Sage

ARNI ME DIOSMO KAI FASCOMILO

◆ ◆ ◆ ◆

This is a traditional Greek pilaf for which lamb or veal can be used.

Preparation time: about 30 minutes
Cooking time: about 1 hour 20 minutes

SERVES: 6−8

- 50 ml/2 fl oz olive oil
- 900 kg/2 lb lean lamb fillet, cut into 2.5 cm/1 in cubes
- 1 onion, chopped
- 2 carrots, diced
- 120 ml/4 fl oz dry white wine
- salt and freshly ground
- black pepper, to taste
- 100 g/4 oz flaked almonds
- 900 ml/1½ pt water
- 225 g/8 oz long-grain rice
- 50 g/2 oz sultanas
- 50 g/2 oz raisins
- ½ tsp dried sage
- 1 tsp dried mint

1 Heat the oil in a large saucepan. Add the cubed meat and cook, turning frequently, until evenly browned. Add the onion and carrots and cook for about 5 minutes. Stir in the wine and season with salt and freshly ground black pepper. Bring to the boil, then cover and cook for 10 minutes.

2 Meanwhile, toast the almonds, either under the grill or in a heavy-based frying pan, until they are golden. Set aside.

3 Stir the water into the meat mixture and continue to simmer for a further 30 minutes, stirring occasionally. Add the rice, sultanas, raisins, sage and mint to the stew and adjust the seasoning, if necessary. Simmer, covered, for a further 30–35 minutes, or until the rice is cooked and the meat is tender, adding a little extra water during cooking if necessary. Scatter the toasted flaked almonds over the stew and serve hot.

Sausage and Pepper Stew
SPETSOFAI

◆ ◆ ◆ ◆

This is a stove-top version of a dish more traditionally cooked in individual clay bowls and baked in the oven. It's simple fare, likely to be served at home or in the country taverns of Greece.

Preparation time: about 15 minutes
Cooking time: about 1 hour 20 minutes
SERVES: 6−8

- 3 tbsp olive oil
- 700 g/1½ lb good quality pork sausages, pricked all over
- 2 onions, sliced into rings
- 5 peppers of various colours, seeded and cut into 1 cm/½ in strips
- 700 g/1½ lb tomatoes, skinned and sliced into rounds
- 3 garlic cloves, crushed
- 2 tsp dried oregano
- 120 ml/4 fl oz dry red wine
- salt and freshly ground black pepper, to taste
- chopped fresh sage, to garnish

1 Heat the oil in a large frying pan and add the sausages, turning them as they cook, until they are evenly browned on all sides. Place the browned sausages on absorbent kitchen paper to drain.

2 Add the onion to the frying pan with the peppers and cook for about 10 minutes, or until softened. Stir in the tomatoes, garlic and oregano.

3 Return the sausages to the pan and add the wine. Season with salt and freshly ground black pepper and simmer, covered, for about 1 hour, or until the sausages are cooked through, adding a little extra water if necessary. Serve sprinkled with chopped fresh sage.

Stewed Steak
SOFRITO

◆ ◆ ◆ ◆

A simple and tasty way to serve beef at the Meze table. This dish is a speciality of the Greek island of Corfu.

Preparation time: about 10 minutes
Cooking time: about 2 hours
SERVES: 6−8

- 1 kg/2¼ lb stewing steak, cut into 1 cm/½ in thick slices
- 4 tbsp plain flour
- salt and freshly ground black pepper, to taste
- 1 tsp dried thyme
- 50 ml/2 fl oz olive oil
- 6 tbsp red wine vinegar
- 6 tbsp water
- 2 garlic cloves, crushed
- 1 tbsp tomato purée
- 2 tbsp chopped fresh parsley, to garnish

1 Place the slices of meat in a mixing bowl and sprinkle over the flour, salt and freshly ground black pepper and the thyme. Toss to coat the meat in the flour mixture.

2 Heat half of the oil in a frying pan and cook half of the meat for about 5 minutes, or until evenly browned, turning and rearranging during cooking. Transfer the browned meat to a plate and add the remaining oil to the frying pan. When hot, fry the remaining meat until evenly browned. Return the first batch of meat to the frying pan.

3 Add the vinegar, water, garlic and tomato purée and stir. Bring to the boil, cover, and simmer for 1−1½ hours, or until the meat is tender and the sauce has thickened. Add a little extra water during cooking if necessary. Sprinkle with chopped parsley to serve.

Beef and Onion Stew

S T E F A D O

This classic stew can also be made with veal.

Preparation time: about 15 minutes
Cooking time: about 2 hours
SERVES: 8–10

- 50 g/2 oz butter
- 1.4 kg/3 lb braising steak, cut into 5 cm/2 in cubes
- 300 ml/½ pt dry red wine
- 400 g/14 oz can chopped tomatoes
- 4 tbsp tomato purée
- 300 ml/½ pt boiling water
- 3 tbsp olive oil
- 3 onions, chopped
- 3 garlic cloves, crushed
- 1 tsp ground cinnamon
- ½ tsp dried oregano
- salt and freshly ground black pepper, to taste
- 4 tbsp chopped fresh parsley, to garnish

1 Melt the butter in a large, heavy saucepan and add the cubed meat. Stir and rearrange the meat to brown evenly on all sides.

2 Add half of the wine and simmer for 5 minutes. Stir in the chopped tomatoes, tomato purée and boiling water. Cover and simmer for 10 minutes.

3 Meanwhile, heat the oil in a frying pan and cook the onions and garlic for about 5 minutes, or until browned. Transfer to the meat in the saucepan and add the cinnamon, oregano, salt and freshly ground black pepper. Cover the stew and simmer over gentle heat for 1–1½ hours or until the meat is very tender, adding the remaining wine during cooking. Sprinkle with chopped fresh parsley to serve.

Lamb Chops with Cheese
ARNI PALIKARI

◆ ◆ ◆ ◆

An unusual but delicious combination of lamb and cheese, cooked in packets of tin foil to retain all of the natural flavours.

Preparation time: about 20 minutes
Cooking time: about 2 hours
Oven temperature: 180°C/350°F/Gas 4

SERVES: 4

- 4 lamb chump chops
- 25 g/1 oz butter
- 1 onion, sliced
- 2 garlic cloves, crushed
- 3 tomatoes, sliced
- 3 tsp dried oregano
- salt and freshly ground black pepper, to taste
- 100 g/4 oz kaseri or Gruyère cheese, sliced thinly

1 Fry the chops, with no extra fat, in a frying pan for about 3 minutes on each side, or until evenly browned. Cut out 4 × 30 cm/12 in square pieces of kitchen foil and place a chop in the centre of each square.

2 Preheat the oven to 180°C/350°F/Gas 4. Melt the butter in the frying pan and sauté the onion and garlic for about 3 minutes. Using a spoon, divide the onion mixture between the lamb chops. Divide the slices of tomato between the packets, placing them on top of the onion mixture. Sprinkle each packet with oregano and season with salt and freshly ground black pepper. Sprinkle the cheese evenly over the four chops.

3 Gather up the sides of each of the pieces of foil and pinch them together in the middle to completely encase the chops. Lift the packets on to a baking sheet in the oven for 1½–2 hours or until the meat is tender and cooked through. Serve in the foil packets.

Lamb Kebabs

SOUVLAKIA

◆ ◆ ◆ ◆

These are small skewers of meat traditionally cooked over charcoal and served as a snack, starter, main course or as part of an array of Meze dishes. The lemon is the secret ingredient in this classic dish, so make sure it is freshly squeezed.

Preparation time: about 20 minutes plus marinating
Cooking time: about 10 minutes
SERVES: 4–6

- 3 tbsp olive oil
- 3 tbsp freshly squeezed lemon juice
- 2 tsp dried thyme
- 2 garlic cloves, crushed
- freshly ground black

- pepper, to taste
- 1 kg/2¼ lb lean lamb, cut into 2.5 cm/1 in cubes
- 6 bay leaves
- wedges of lemon, to serve

1 To make the marinade; mix together the olive oil, lemon juice, thyme, garlic and freshly ground black pepper in a screw-top jar. Secure the lid and shake well to combine the ingredients.

2 Place the cubed lamb in a shallow dish. Crumble 2 bay leaves and sprinkle over the meat. Pour the marinade over the meat and stir to coat evenly. Cover and refrigerate for 2 hours.

3 Thread the remaining bay leaves on to four metal skewers, then divide the meat between them. Cook the kebabs under a preheated grill for about 5–10 minutes, or until they are cooked through. Brush with the reserved marinade and turn the kebabs during cooking. Serve with the lemon wedges.

Fresh Ham Macaroni

HIRINO YAHNI MAKARONADA

◆ ◆ ◆ ◆

A simple Greek recipe with a definite Italian influence.

Preparation time: about 30 minutes
Cooking time: about 3 hours
SERVES: 10–12

- 100 g/4 oz butter
- 700 g/1½ lb piece of ham, cut into 5 cm/2 in cubes
- salt and freshly ground black pepper, to taste
- ½ tsp ground cinnamon
- 1 large onion, chopped
- 8 tbsp tomato purée

- 1.2 l/2 pt boiling water
- 1 cinnamon stick
- 450 g/1 lb dried macaroni
- 225 g/8 oz kefalotyri or fresh parmesan cheese, grated, to serve

1 Melt half of the butter in a large frying pan and add the cubed ham. Season with salt and freshly ground black pepper and add the ground cinnamon. Cook the ham, turning and rearranging frequently, for about 5 minutes, or until the meat is evenly browned.

2 Melt half of the remaining butter in a large saucepan and add the onion. Cook for 5–7 minutes, or until golden. Add the browned meat mixture to the saucepan, with the tomato purée, boiling water and cinnamon stick. Simmer, uncovered, for 2–2½ hours, or until the sauce is slightly thickened and the meat is tender.

3 Cook the macaroni in a large saucepan of boiling water until tender. Drain and turn into a warm serving platter. Cover with kitchen foil to keep warm. Melt the remaining butter in a small frying pan and cook for about 3 minutes, or until browned. Pour over the macaroni, then sprinkle the grated cheese over the top. Pour the ham sauce evenly over the macaroni and serve.

Lamb Cooked in Foil

ARNI KLEFTIKO

◆ ◆ ◆ ◆

Authentic Greek *Kleftiko* is cooked to the point where the meat just falls off the bone. The secret is long, slow cooking in a foil parcel to allow the flavours to stay trapped inside until the meat is so tender that it literally melts in the mouth. A large wedge of lemon is served with the meat to help cleanse the palate.

Preparation time: about 10 minutes
Cooking time: about 2 hours
Oven temperature: 180°C/350°F/Gas 4

SERVES: 8

- *8 lamb chops*
- *4 garlic cloves, cut into slivers*
- *50 g/2 oz butter, melted*
- *3 tbsp freshly squeezed*
- *lemon juice*
- *salt and freshly ground black pepper, to taste*
- *1 tbsp dried oregano*
- *1 tbsp dried mint*

1 Preheat the oven to 180°C/350°F/Gas 4. Using a small, sharp knife, make incisions in the chops and insert the slivers of garlic into them. Place each chop in the centre of a 30 cm/12 in square piece of kitchen foil.

2 Distribute the remaining ingredients between the four chops and gather up the foil, pinching it together at the top to completely encase and seal in the chops.

3 Arrange the parcels on a baking sheet and cook for 1½–2 hours, or until the meat is cooked through and very tender. Serve the parcels closed.

Minced Meat Kebabs

KOFTA

◆ ◆ ◆ ◆

The ingredients for *Kofta* vary from house to house and from region to region. Here is a recipe to guide you towards finding your own variation for this favourite Greek dish.

Preparation time: about 15 minutes
Cooking time: about 10 minutes
SERVES: 8−10

- 900 g/2 lb minced lamb, beef or a mixture of both
- 2 onions, minced or grated
- 1 tsp ground cinnamon
- 1 tsp paprika
- 1 tsp ground cumin
- 1 tsp ground coriander
- 2 tbsp very finely chopped fresh parsley
- 2 garlic cloves, crushed
- olive oil, for greasing

1 Place all the ingredients in a large mixing bowl and mix thoroughly to combine.

2 Divide the mixture between metal skewers, shaping the mixture around them to form a sausage shape. Lightly oil the grill rack to prevent the kebabs from sticking. Cook under a high heat for 5−10 minutes, or until the meat is browned and cooked through, turning and rearranging during cooking. Serve with fresh pitta bread, a selection of salads and lemon wedges, if you wish.

Chicken Meze

Grilled Chicken with Greek Yoghurt

◆

Garlic Chicken on a Stick

◆

Chicken Oregano

◆

Lemon Chicken

◆

Chicken with Macaroni

◆

Fried Chicken Balls

◆

Skewered Chicken

◆

Chicken with Feta and Green Olives

◆

Chicken and Tomato Casserole

◆

Chicken Wings with Lime Juice and Garlic

◆

Chicken and Potato Casserole

◆

Chicken Roasted with Pistachios

◆

Chicken Pie

◆

Roasted Chicken with Vegetables

◆

Chicken Pilaf

Grilled Chicken with Greek Yoghurt

KOTOPOULO YIAOURTI

Chicken legs are used in this recipe, but other chicken portions work equally well. The yoghurt is used not only for flavour but also to tenderize the meat, making it more succulent and juicy.

Preparation time: about 10 minutes plus marinating
Cooking time: about 20–40 minutes

SERVES: 6

- 6 chicken legs
- 3 garlic cloves, crushed
- salt and freshly ground black pepper, to taste
- 1 tsp paprika
- 1 tsp ground cinnamon
- pinch of cayenne pepper
- freshly squeezed juice of 1 lemon
- 8 tbsp olive oil
- 8 tbsp Greek yoghurt
- lemon wedges, to serve

1 Place the chicken legs in a large, shallow dish. In a medium-sized bowl, combine the garlic, salt and freshly ground black pepper, paprika, cinnamon, cayenne pepper, lemon juice, oil and Greek yoghurt.

2 Pour the marinade over the chicken legs, stirring and turning them to coat evenly. Cover and leave to marinate in the refrigerator for 2–3 hours or overnight.

3 Season the chicken legs again with plenty of salt and freshly ground black pepper. Place the chicken legs on an oiled grill rack under a preheated grill and cook for 20–40 minutes or until crisp and golden on the outside and cooked through, turning frequently during cooking. Serve with lemon wedges.

Garlic Chicken on a Stick
KOTA ME SKORTHO

❖ ❖ ❖

A handy tip is to soak the wooden skewers in lemon juice for 30 minutes before using them. This gives a lovely tangy flavour to the chicken and helps to prevent the sticks from burning under the grill.

Preparation time: about 20 minutes plus marinating
Cooking time: about 5–10 minutes

SERVES: 6

- *6 chicken breasts, skinned and boned*
- *6 garlic cloves, crushed*
- *salt and freshly ground black pepper, to taste*
- *freshly squeezed juice of 2 lemons*
- *8 tbsp olive oil*
- *6 tbsp very finely chopped fresh parsley*

1 Cut the chicken fillets into 2.5 cm/1 in pieces and place in a shallow dish.

2 In a small bowl, mix together the garlic, salt and freshly ground black pepper, lemon juice and olive oil. Pour the marinade over the chicken pieces, stir, cover and marinate for 2–4 hours in the refrigerator, turning and rearranging them occasionally.

3 Spread the chopped parsley out on a plate. Divide the chicken pieces into six equal portions and thread on to six wooden skewers. Roll each skewer in the chopped parsley to coat evenly.

4 Arrange the chicken skewers on an oiled grill rack and cook under a preheated grill for 5–10 minutes or until the chicken is golden on the outside and cooked through. Turn and rearrange the skewers, basting them with the remaining marinade during cooking for an even more delicious result.

Chicken Oregano

KOTOPOULO RIGANATO TIS SKARAS

This simple, tasty dish is perfect for the barbecue on a hot summer's day, or grilled for a fast Meze dish.

Preparation time: about 10 minutes plus marinating
Cooking time: about 30 minutes
SERVES: 6—8

- 6–8 chicken portions
- 120 ml/4 fl oz olive oil
- 120 ml/4 fl oz dry white wine
- 2 tbsp dried oregano
- salt and freshly ground black pepper, to taste
- 2 garlic cloves, crushed

1 Arrange the chicken portions in a large, shallow dish.

2 In a small bowl, combine the oil, wine, oregano, salt and freshly ground black pepper and the garlic. Mix well. Spread the marinade over the chicken portions, cover, and marinate for 2–3 hours, turning and re-arranging occasionally.

3 Place the chicken portions on an oiled grill rack and cook under a preheated grill for about 30 minutes or until the chicken is crisp and golden on the outside and cooked through, turning and rearranging several times during cooking. Serve warm or cold.

Quick and Easy Menu

Classic Greek Salad
Horiatiki Salata

◆

Chickpea Dip
Hummus

◆

Roasted Chicken with Vegetables
Kota me Ladera

◆

Minced Meat Kebabs
Kofta

◆

Pitta Bread

◆

Almond Cakes
Pastoules

◆

Wine: Santorin
(Crisp white wine)

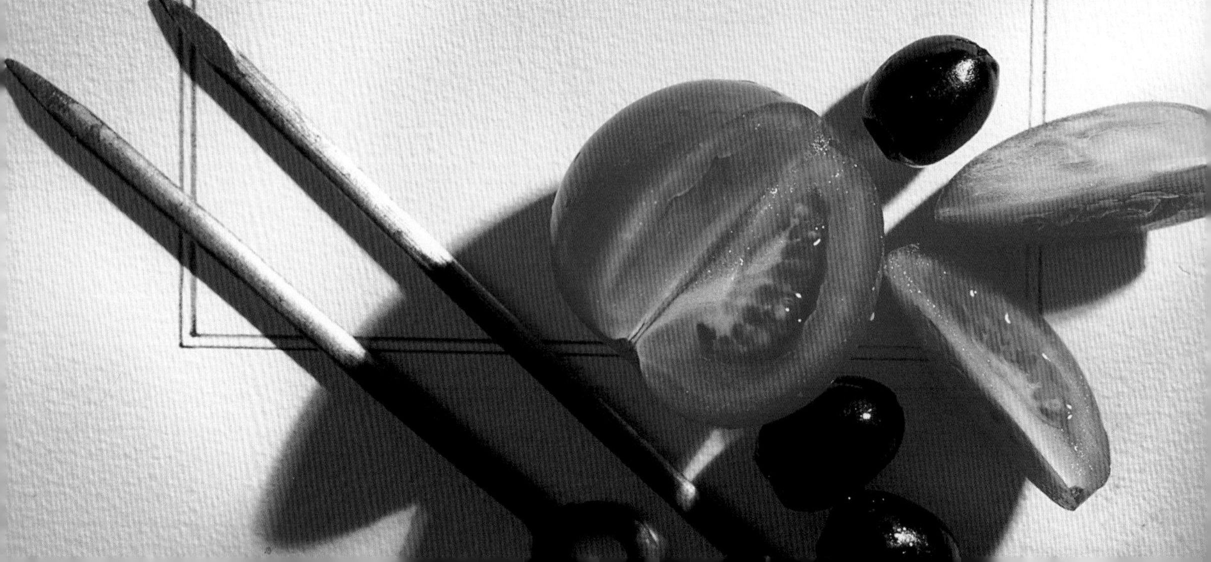

◆

Lemon Chicken

KOTOPOULO ME AVGOLEMONO

Chicken flavoured with lemon is such a delicious combination of tastes and one that is commonly found in Greece. There is plenty of sauce in this dish so rice would be a welcome accompaniment.

Preparation time: about 20 minutes
Cooking time: about 45 minutes
SERVES: 6–8

- *1.6 kg/3½ lb prepared chicken, without giblets, cut into small portions*
- *50 g/2 oz butter*
- *salt and freshly ground black pepper, to taste*
- *300 ml/½ pt boiling water*
- *1 bunch spring onions, trimmed and cut into 2.5 cm/1 in pieces*
- *3 eggs*
- *3 tbsp freshly squeezed lemon juice*
- *2 tbsp chopped fresh dill, to garnish*

1 Melt the butter in a large, heavy-based saucepan and add the chicken. Cook for about 5 minutes, or until evenly browned, turning and rearranging during cooking.

2 Season the chicken with salt and freshly ground black pepper and add the boiling water and the spring onions. Cover and simmer for 35–40 minutes, or until the chicken is tender and cooked through.

3 Place the eggs in a small bowl and beat well. Gradually whisk in the lemon juice, a little at a time to prevent curdling. Whisk in 300 ml/½ pt of the cooking liquid from the chicken. Pour the egg and lemon mixture over the chicken and stir continuously until the sauce has thickened slightly. Do not boil.

4 Transfer the chicken and sauce to a warm serving dish and sprinkle with the chopped fresh dill.

Chicken with Macaroni

KOTA KAPAMA

Make the sauce in advance and keep refrigerated until required. The sauce can be reheated while the macaroni is cooking and you have a substantial dish which has taken you no time at all to prepare to add to the Meze table.

Preparation time: about 20 minutes
Cooking time: about 1 hour 15 minutes
SERVES: 6–8

- 900 g/2 lb chicken thighs, skinned
- salt and freshly ground black pepper, to taste
- pinch of ground cinnamon
- 75 g/3 oz butter
- 2 × 400 g/14 oz can chopped tomatoes
- 8 tbsp tomato purée
- 1 tsp sugar
- 175 ml/6 fl oz boiling water
- 2 cinnamon sticks
- 1 onion, grated
- 2 garlic cloves, crushed
- 450 g/1 lb macaroni
- 225 g/8 oz kefalotyri or fresh parmesan cheese, grated

1 Arrange the chicken thighs on a chopping board and sprinkle evenly with salt and freshly ground black pepper and cinnamon.

2 Melt half the butter in a large, heavy-based saucepan and sauté the chicken on all sides for about 5 minutes, or until evenly browned.

3 Add the chopped tomatoes, tomato purée, sugar and boiling water to the chicken. Stir and add the cinnamon sticks. Cook over gentle heat for 5 minutes.

4 Melt the remaining butter in a frying pan and sauté the onion and garlic for 3–5 minutes or until softened. Add to the chicken mixture and increase the heat to bring to the boil. Cover and simmer for about 1 hour, or until the chicken is tender and the sauce has thickened, stirring occasionally.

5 In the last 20 minutes of the cooking time, cook the macaroni in a large saucepan of boiling water until tender. Drain under hot running water then turn out on to a warm serving platter. Pour the chicken sauce over the macaroni and sprinkle the grated cheese over the top. Serve immediately.

Fried Chicken Balls

KOTO TIGHANITO

The chicken mixture in this recipe could be formed into sausage shapes around skewers and grilled or barbecued to be served as chicken *Koftas*.

Preparation time: about 15 minutes
Cooking time: about 8 minutes
SERVES: 6–8

- 3 chicken breasts, skinned, boned and finely minced
- 50 g/2 oz fresh white breadcrumbs
- 50 g/2 oz pine nuts, ground
- 3 tbsp finely chopped fresh parsley
- ½ tsp ground turmeric
- 1 egg, beaten
- salt and freshly ground black pepper, to taste
- flour, for dredging
- olive oil, for shallow frying
- freshly squeezed juice of 1 lemon

1 Place the chicken in a mixing bowl and add the breadcrumbs, pine nuts, parsley and turmeric. Mix well to combine.

2 Add the beaten egg to the chicken mixture and season with salt and freshly ground black pepper. With slightly damp hands, shape the chicken mixture into balls the size of walnuts and place on a baking sheet lined with greaseproof paper.

3 Sprinkle the balls lightly with flour. Heat the oil in a deep non-stick frying pan and fry the chicken balls, a few at a time, for about 5–8 minutes or until crisp and cooked through, turning them to ensure they cook evenly. Transfer the cooked chicken balls to an ovenproof dish and place in a low oven to keep warm while the remaining batches are cooked. Serve warm or cold, sprinkled with lemon juice.

Skewered Chicken

SOUVLAKIA ME KOTA

This classic Greek dish should be served at the Meze table with plenty of garlicky *Tzatziki* and warm pitta bread.

Preparation time: about 20 minutes plus marinating
Cooking time: about 20–25 minutes

SERVES: 6

- 120 ml/4 fl oz olive oil
- 1 tbsp freshly squeezed lemon juice
- 1 tbsp wine vinegar
- 50 ml/2 fl oz dry red wine
- 2 garlic cloves, crushed
- 1 tsp dried mint
- 4 chicken breasts, skinned, boned and cut into 2.5 cm/1 in cubes
- 225 g/8 oz chicken livers, cut into small pieces
- 2 green peppers, seeded and cut into chunks
- 12 medium-sized mushrooms, cleaned
- 12 cherry tomatoes

1 In a small bowl, combine the oil, lemon juice, wine vinegar, red wine, garlic and mint. Mix well.

2 Arrange the chicken breasts and chicken livers in a shallow dish. Pour the marinade over the chicken and stir to coat. Cover and marinate in the refrigerator for 2–3 hours, stirring occasionally.

3 Thread the chicken, chicken livers, peppers, mushrooms and cherry tomatoes alternately and equally on to six metal skewers. Brush with any remaining marinade and place on an oiled grill rack under a preheated grill. Cook for 20–25 minutes or until crisp and cooked through, turning and rearranging during cooking.

Chicken with Feta and Green Olives

KOTO BARTHOUNIKIOTOU

✦ ✦ ✦ ✦

This dish originates from a small village called Barthouna, near Sparta. It is either prepared with olives or raisins, both being major products of this region.

Preparation time: about 30 minutes
Cooking time: about 40 minutes
SERVES: 4

- *4 chicken breasts*
- *flour, for dredging*
- *salt and freshly ground black pepper, to taste*
- *6 tbsp olive oil*
- *350 g/12 oz button onions (or use large onions, quartered)*
- *400 g/14 oz can chopped tomatoes*
- *120 ml/4 fl oz boiling water*
- *275 g/10 oz pitted green olives, washed and drained*
- *1 tbsp red wine vinegar*
- *100 g/4 oz feta cheese, sliced thinly*

1 Arrange the chicken breasts on a chopping board, dredge with the flour and season with salt and freshly ground black pepper on both sides.

2 Heat the oil in a large, deep frying pan and add the chicken breasts, skin-side down. Cook on both sides for 3–5 minutes or until browned. Lift the chicken breasts out of the pan and set aside.

3 Add the onions to the frying pan and sauté for about 5 minutes or until softened, stirring frequently. Return the chicken to the pan and add the chopped tomatoes and boiling water. Season with salt and freshly ground black pepper, cover, and simmer for 25–30 minutes or until the chicken is tender and cooked through, adding a little extra boiling water if necessary.

4 In the last 10 minutes of the cooking time, add the green olives and red wine vinegar. Stir to combine. Place a slice of feta cheese on top of each piece of chicken and continue to cook, uncovered, for a further 10 minutes, or until the cheese has just melted. Serve immediately.

Chicken and Tomato Casserole

KOTOPOULO KOKKINISTO

❖ ❖ ❖ ❖

Kokkinisto is the name generally given to any meat which is casseroled in a rich tomato sauce.

Preparation time: about 15 minutes
Cooking time: about 1 hour 15 minutes
Oven temperature: 190°C/375°F/Gas 5
SERVES: 4–6

- 50 ml/2 fl oz olive oil
- 1.6 kg/3½ lb prepared chicken, cut into portions
- flour, for dredging
- 2 large red onions, sliced
- 2 × 400 g/14 oz cans chopped tomatoes
- 3 garlic cloves, crushed
- salt and freshly ground black pepper, to taste
- 85 ml/3 fl oz boiling water
- 2 tbsp red wine vinegar
- chopped fresh parsley, to garnish

1 Preheat the oven to 190°C/375°F/Gas 5. Heat the oil in a large, flameproof casserole. Place the chicken portions on a chopping board and dredge all over with flour. Place in the casserole and cook for about 5 minutes, or until evenly browned, turning the portions as they cook. Using a slotted spoon, transfer the chicken portions to a plate and set aside.

2 Add the onion to the casserole and cook for 3 minutes, or until softened. Return the chicken to the casserole, add the chopped tomatoes and garlic and season with salt and freshly ground black pepper. Add the boiling water, cover, and cook in the oven for 45–55 minutes or until the chicken is tender and the sauce has thickened.

3 In the last 5 minutes of cooking time, stir in the red wine vinegar and a little extra boiling water if necessary. Serve sprinkled with chopped fresh parsley.

Chicken Wings with Lime Juice and Garlic

KOTOPOULO MARINATO

• • • •

Whenever you buy a whole chicken, freeze the wings if they are not needed. When you have enough collected in the freezer you can transform them into this deliciously tangy recipe.

Preparation time: about 10 minutes plus marinating
Cooking time: about 25 minutes

SERVES: 8–12

- *12 chicken wings*
- *4 garlic cloves, crushed*
- *salt and freshly ground black pepper, to taste*
- *freshly squeezed juice of 4 limes*
- *pinch of cayenne pepper*

1 Place the chicken wings in a shallow dish. Rub the crushed garlic all over the chicken wings, then season with salt and freshly ground black pepper.

2 Sprinkle the lime juice and cayenne pepper over the chicken wings, cover, and marinate in the refrigerator for 3–4 hours, turning and rearranging them occasionally.

3 Arrange the chicken wings in a large frying pan and pour the marinade over them. Add just enough cold water to cover the wings and bring quickly to the boil. Simmer gently for 20–25 minutes, or until the chicken is cooked through and the sauce has reduced slightly. Serve warm or, better still, cold the next day.

Chicken and Potato Casserole

KOTOPOULO ME PATATES

✦ ✦ ✦ ✦

If you prefer you can use boned chicken portions in this recipe – less authentic, but just as tasty.

Preparation time: about 20 minutes
Cooking time: about 2 hours
SERVES: 4–6

- *1.6 kg/3½ lb prepared chicken, without giblets, cut into small portions*
- *freshly squeezed juice of 1 lemon*
- *2 tbsp olive oil*
- *2 onions, finely chopped*
- *1 red pepper, seeded and finely chopped*
- *4 large tomatoes, skinned, seeded and chopped*
- *900 ml/1½ pt boiling*
- *water*
- *1 tbsp tomato purée*
- *2 garlic cloves, crushed*
- *3 bay leaves, crushed*
- *4 tbsp chopped fresh parsley*
- *2 medium-sized potatoes, peeled and cut into chunks*
- *pinch of sugar*
- *salt and freshly ground black pepper, to taste*
- *chopped fresh parsley, to garnish*

1 Lay the chicken portions out on a chopping board and sprinkle with lemon juice. Heat the olive oil in a large, heavy-based saucepan and sauté the chicken pieces for 5–10 minutes or until evenly browned, turning during cooking. Add the onions and cook for a further 5 minutes or until softened.

2 Add the red pepper and tomatoes and cook for 3–4 minutes. Add the boiling water to the saucepan and return to the boil. Add the tomato purée, garlic, bay leaves, parsley, potatoes and sugar, and season with salt and freshly ground black pepper. Stir, cover, and simmer for about 1½ hours or until the chicken is cooked through and the potatoes are tender. Sprinkle with a little extra chopped parsley to serve.

BELOW
In contrast to sun-seeking tourists, elderly Greek locals wisely head for the shade in high summer.

Chicken Roasted with Pistachios

KOTOPOULO ME PISTACHIO

This is a variation of one of Greece's most popular dishes. The chicken should be cut up into pieces and served with the stuffing separately at the Meze table.

Preparation time: about 25 minutes
Cooking time: about 2 hours
Oven temperature: 230°C/450°F/Gas 8
then 180°C/350°F/Gas 4
SERVES: 6—8

- 50 ml/2 fl oz olive oil
- 2 onions, finely chopped
- 225 g/8 oz long-grain rice
- 4 large tomatoes, skinned, seeded and chopped
- 225 g/8 oz shelled pistachio nuts, roughly chopped
- 100 g/4 oz seedless raisins
- pinch of ground cinnamon
- salt and freshly ground black pepper, to taste
- 525 ml/18 fl oz boiling water
- 3 tbsp very finely chopped fresh parsley
- 1.6 kg/3½ lb prepared chicken, without giblets
- 50 ml/2 fl oz dry white wine

1 Preheat the oven to 230°C/450°F/Gas 8. Heat half of the olive oil in a large, heavy frying pan and sauté the onion for about 5 minutes or until softened.

2 Add the rice to the frying pan and continue to cook for a further 3 minutes or until the rice begins to brown, stirring occasionally. Add half of the tomatoes, the pistachios, raisins, cinnamon, salt and freshly ground black pepper and 175 ml/6 fl oz boiling water. Simmer for about 10 minutes or until the liquid is mostly absorbed and the rice is almost cooked, stirring continuously. Remove from the heat and stir in the parsley.

3 Spoon the rice mixture into the cavity of the chicken without packing it too firmly. Place the chicken in a roasting tin and spoon any remaining rice mixture around

the outside. Season the chicken with salt and freshly ground black pepper.

4 Scatter the remaining chopped tomatoes around the chicken and pour 350 ml/12 fl oz boiling water and the wine into the tin. Reduce the oven temperature to 180°C/350°F/Gas 4. In this way the chicken skin is seared and made crispy before the oven adjusts to the lower heat. Drizzle the remaining olive oil over the chicken and roast for about 1½ hours or until the chicken is cooked through and the rice, inside and outside of the chicken, is tender. The chicken should be basted several times during cooking and a little extra water may be added if necessary. Allow the chicken to stand for 10 minutes before cutting into portions and serving with the stuffing.

Chicken Pie
KOTOPITTA

This pie is perfect fare for summertime entertaining outside. Delicious hot or cold, it's easy to make and always looks impressive.

Preparation time: about 45 minutes
Cooking time: about 50 minutes
Oven temperature: 180°C/350°F/Gas 4
SERVES: 8—10

- *120 ml/4 fl oz olive oil*
- *6 sheets of filo pastry, thawed if frozen*
- *2 chicken breasts, skinned, boned and cut into small pieces*
- *1 bunch of spring onions, chopped*
- *3 tbsp chopped fresh dill*
- *2 celery sticks, finely chopped*
- *salt and freshly ground black pepper, to taste*

- *2 tsp dried thyme*
- *1 tsp dried mint*
- *½ tsp dried marjoram*
- *½ tsp dried tarragon*
- *175 g/6 oz feta cheese, crumbled*
- *2 tbsp grated kefalotyri or fresh parmesan cheese*
- *2 eggs, lightly beaten*
- *½ tsp ouzo (optional)*
- *1 egg yolk, beaten, to glaze*

1 Preheat the oven to 180°C/350°F/Gas 4. Grease a 25 cm/10 in pie dish with some of the olive oil. Lay the filo pastry out on the work surface and cover with a slightly damp cloth to prevent it from drying out.

2 Place the chicken breasts in a large mixing bowl with the spring onions, dill, celery, salt and freshly ground black pepper and herbs. Scatter in the crumbled feta and the grated cheese and mix thoroughly to combine. Add the beaten eggs, ouzo, if using, 2 tbsp olive oil and mix.

3 Separate one sheet of filo pastry from the rest and lay it on the work surface, keeping the remaining sheets covered with the cloth. Brush the separated sheet with some of the olive oil, then lay another sheet of filo pastry on top. Brush with oil and repeat with a third layer of pastry. Brush again with olive oil, then lay the oiled sheets in the base of the pie dish, allowing the excess pastry to hang over the edges of the plate.

4 Spoon the chicken mixture into the lined pie dish and spread it out evenly. Repeat the brushing and layering process with the remaining sheets of pastry, then lay them on top of the chicken filling.

5 Roll the edges of the filo pastry together to firmly seal in the filling and make a few small incisions in the top of the pie to allow the steam to escape during cooking. Brush with the beaten egg yolk to glaze and bake for 45–50 minutes or until the pastry is crisp and the chicken is cooked through. Serve warm or cold, cut into slices.

Roasted Chicken with Vegetables

KOTA ME LADERA

The vegetables in this recipe can be your own choice, but remember the softer the raw vegetable the less time it will need to cook; so adjust the cooking times accordingly.

Preparation time: about 15 minutes
Cooking time: about 2 hours
Oven temperature: 230°C/450°F/Gas 8
then 180°C/350°F/Gas 4

SERVES: 6−8

- 6–8 chicken portions
- 85 ml/3 fl oz olive oil
- salt and freshly ground black pepper, to taste
- freshly squeezed juice of 2 lemons
- 2 tsp dried thyme
- ½ tsp dried marjoram
- 3 garlic cloves, finely chopped
- 2 large potatoes, peeled and cut lengthways into wedges
- 3 carrots, cut into large chunks
- 1 red pepper, seeded and quartered
- 1 green pepper, seeded and quartered
- 6–8 cup mushrooms, cleaned
- 3 medium-sized courgettes, cut into large chunks

1 Preheat the oven to 230°C/450°F/Gas 8. Place the chicken portions in a large roasting tin and rub them all over with 2 tbsp of the olive oil. Season with salt and freshly ground black pepper.

2 In a small bowl, combine the remaining olive oil, lemon juice, thyme, marjoram, garlic and some more freshly ground black pepper. Mix well and brush evenly over the chicken portions.

3 Scatter the vegetables around in the roasting tin and season with salt and freshly ground black pepper. Reduce the oven temperature to 180°C/350°F/Gas 4: the chicken skin will go crispy before the oven temperature reduces. Add the boiling water to the roasting tin and cook for about 2 hours or until the chicken is cooked through and the vegetables are tender and crisp, basting the chicken and vegetables frequently during cooking. Serve warm.

BELOW
Early summer, and a poppy field adds a splash of colour to the parched Plain of Lesithi.

Chicken Pilaf
K O T O P O U L O   P I L A F I

The classic Greek way to finish preparing this dish, and also many others which use pasta or rice, is to brown some butter in a small pan and pour it over just before serving. It's an optional stage in this version, and if you are particularly worried about your fat intake you might like to leave it out.

Preparation time: about 10 minutes
Cooking time: about 45 minutes
SERVES: 6−8

- *100 g/4 oz butter*
- *900 g/2 lb chicken breasts, skinned, boned and cut into bite-sized pieces*
- *salt and freshly ground black pepper, to taste*
- *pinch of ground cinnamon*
- *pinch of ground allspice*
- *2 onions, chopped*
- *3 tbsp tomato purée*
- *600 ml/1 pt boiling water*
- *225 g/8 oz long-grain rice*
- *50 g/2 oz butter*
- *chopped fresh mint, to garnish*

1 Melt the butter in a large, heavy-based saucepan and sauté the chicken pieces for 5–10 minutes or until lightly browned, turning during cooking. Add the salt and freshly ground black pepper, cinnamon and allspice, and stir well.

2 Add the onions to the saucepan and continue to cook until softened. Stir in the tomato purée and boiling water. Cover and cook for 20 minutes; then add the rice. Cover and continue to simmer for a further 20–25 minutes or until the chicken is cooked through and the rice is tender.

3 Remove the cover for the final 10 minutes of the cooking time to allow the liquid to be absorbed. Melt the butter in a small frying pan and cook until browned. Turn the pilaf out on to a warm serving platter and pour the browned butter over the top. Sprinkle with chopped fresh mint to serve.

Fish Meze

Fish Fillets with Feta and Tomatoes

◆

Fried Seafood

◆

Fish Baked in Wine

◆

Deep-fried Squid

◆

Prawn Bake

◆

Deep-fried Cod's Roe

◆

Red Mullet with Garlic

◆

Fish and Vegetable Casserole

◆

Stuffed Fish Fillets with Egg and Lemon Sauce

◆

Salt Cod Fritters with Garlic

◆

Deep-fried Mussels

◆

Swordfish Kebabs

◆

Small Fish in Vine Leaves

◆

Prawn Pilaf

◆

Sardines Cooked with Tomatoes and Rosemary

Fish Fillets with Feta and Tomatoes
FETES PSARI ME FETA KAI DOMATES

❖ ❖ ❖ ❖

The Greeks hold their seas and the living creatures within them in high esteem and it is not their way to smother a fish in strongly flavoured sauces or to cook it for any great length of time. They eat the freshest of seafood with the minimum of cooking in order that the delicate flavours and textures remain the central features of the dish.

Preparation time: about 10 minutes
Cooking time: about 5–10 minutes
SERVES: 6–8

- 900 g/2 lb flounder fillets, skinned
- olive oil, for greasing
- 1 large onion, grated
- salt and freshly ground black pepper, to taste
- 4 tomatoes, skinned, seeded and chopped
- 100 g/4 oz butter, melted
- 175 g/6 oz feta cheese, crumbled
- chopped fresh parsley, to garnish

1 Arrange the fish fillets in a single layer in an oiled, large, shallow, flameproof dish.

2 Scatter the onion over the fish fillets and season with the salt and freshly ground black pepper. Scatter the chopped tomato over the onion and fish.

3 Drizzle half of the melted butter over the fish fillets and place under a preheated grill for 5–7 minutes. Drizzle over the remaining melted butter and sprinkle over the feta cheese. Continue to cook for a further 3–5 minutes, or until the fish flakes easily and is cooked through. Sprinkle with chopped fresh parsley to serve.

TOP
Red mullet, chicken kebabs, octopus, Mediterranean shrimps and snapper tempt passers-by at a stall on Réthimnon harbour.

Fried Seafood
OSTRAKA

◆ ◆ ◆ ◆

This simple but delicious Meze dish should be served with plenty of fresh lemon wedges.

Preparation time: about 10 minutes
Cooking time: about 5–10 minutes
SERVES: 8–10

- 900 g/2 lb prepared mixed seafood (including peeled prawns, sliced squid, chunks of skinned white fish fillets, whitebait)
- flour, for coating
- salt and freshly ground
- black pepper, to taste
- olive oil, for shallow frying
- freshly squeezed juice of 1 lemon
- lemon wedges, to serve

1 Place the prepared seafood in a large mixing bowl and sprinkle over enough flour to coat the seafood lightly and evenly. Toss gently.

2 Season the floured fish with salt and freshly ground black pepper. Heat the oil in a deep frying pan and fry the seafood in batches for 5–7 minutes or until golden and cooked through. Using a slotted spoon, transfer to a dish lined with absorbent kitchen paper to drain.

3 Spinkle the fried seafood with the lemon juice and serve warm with the extra lemon wedges.

Fish Baked in Wine
PSARI PLAKI

◆ ◆ ◆ ◆

Plaki is the Greek word given to the method of cooking in this recipe. It can also be applied to dishes cooked with beans or vegetables in the same manner.

Preparation time: about 15 minutes
Cooking time: about 55 minutes
Oven temperature: 180°C/350°F/Gas 4
SERVES: 8–10

- 120 ml/4 fl oz olive oil
- 2 large onions, sliced into rings
- 4 sticks of celery, roughly chopped
- 4 spring onions, chopped
- 4 tbsp chopped fresh parsley
- 4 tomatoes, sliced
- 3 garlic cloves, crushed
- 900 g/2 lb sea bass fillets, skinned
- 2 tsp dried oregano
- salt and freshly ground black pepper, to taste
- 2 lemons, thinly sliced
- 300 ml/½ pt dry white wine
- 3 tbsp freshly squeezed lemon juice
- 75 g/3 oz fresh white breadcrumbs
- chopped fresh parsley, to garnish

1 Preheat the oven to 180°C/350°F/Gas 4. Heat all but 2 tbsp of the olive oil in a frying pan and sauté the onion for about 3 minutes or until softened. Add the celery, spring onions, parsley, tomatoes and garlic. Stir gently and continue to cook for a further 5 minutes.

2 Grease a large, shallow ovenproof dish with the remaining oil and arrange the fish fillets in it. Sprinkle the oregano over the fish and season with salt and freshly ground black pepper. Spoon the cooked onion mixture evenly over the fish and scatter over the slices of lemon.

3 Pour in the wine and the lemon juice and spinkle over the breadcrumbs. Bake, uncovered, for about 45 minutes, or until the fish flakes easily and the topping is golden. Sprinkle with chopped fresh parsley to serve.

Deep-fried Squid
KALAMARIA TIGANITA

◆ ◆ ◆ ◆

This is a well-known classic of the Greek Meze table, a favourite summer dish.

Preparation time: about 20 minutes
Cooking time: about 5–10 minutes
SERVES: 8–10

- 900 g/2 lb small fresh squid, cleaned and cut into 1 cm/½ in rings
- flour, for coating
- salt and freshly ground
- black pepper, to taste
- vegetable oil, for deep-fat frying
- lemon wedges, to serve

1 Place the squid in a large mixing bowl. Sprinkle over enough flour to coat the squid rings lightly and evenly. Season with salt and freshly ground black pepper and toss lightly.

2 Heat the oil and fry the squid in batches for about 3-5 minutes or until crisp, golden and cooked through. Using a slotted spoon, transfer to a dish lined with absorbent kitchen paper to drain. Serve with the lemon wedges.

Prawn Bake

GARIDES ME SALTSA

✦ ✦ ✦ ✦

This dish is far better without the extra addition of salt during cooking, as this tends to toughen the delicate texture of the prawns. If you find that the salt from the feta cheese is not sufficient for your taste, then only add more at the table.

Preparation time: about 10 minutes
Cooking time: about 45 minutes
Oven temperature: 220°C/425°F/Gas 7
SERVES: 6—8

- 3 tbsp olive oil
- 2 large onions, grated
- 2 garlic cloves, crushed
- 3 tbsp chopped fresh parsley
- 1 tbsp chopped fresh dill
- pinch of dry mustard powder
- pinch of sugar
- 400 g/14 oz can chopped tomatoes
- 1 tbsp tomato purée
- 450 g/1 lb fresh prawns, shelled and deveined
- 225 g/8 oz feta cheese, crumbled
- chopped fresh dill, to garnish

1 Heat the olive oil in a large saucepan and sauté the onions for about 5 minutes, or until softened and beginning to brown. Add the garlic, chopped fresh herbs, mustard powder, sugar, chopped tomatoes and tomato purée. Simmer the mixture, uncovered, for about 30 minutes, or until the sauce has reduced and thickened slighly. In the mean time, preheat the oven to 220°C/425°F/Gas 7.

2 Add the prawns to the sauce and stir. Continue to cook for a further 3–5 minutes, or until all the prawns have turned pink and are cooked through.

3 Pour the mixture into an ovenproof serving dish and scatter over the crumbled feta cheese. Bake for about 5–10 minutes, or until the cheese has melted. Serve immediately, sprinkled with chopped fresh dill.

Deep-fried Cod's Roe
TARAMA KEFTEDES

◆ ◆ ◆ ◆

Outside Greece we tend to think of smoked cod's roe as being used for *Taramosalata* alone. In fact it is used for several dishes, many of which you would find on the Meze table, including this one.

Preparation time: about 20 minutes plus chilling
Cooking time: about 5–10 minutes
SERVES: 8–10

- 450 g/1 lb smoked cod's roe
- 1 onion, chopped
- 75 g/3 oz fresh white breadcrumbs
- 2 tbsp freshly squeezed lemon juice
- 3 garlic cloves, crushed
- freshly ground black pepper, to taste
- 5 tbsp chopped fresh parsley
- 2 egg whites, lightly beaten
- flour, for coating
- olive oil, for shallow frying
- lemon wedges, to serve

1 Peel the membrane away from the cod's roe and discard. Place the roe in a food processor or blender with the breadcrumbs, lemon juice, garlic, freshly ground black pepper and parsley. Purée until smooth, adding a little of the egg white to soften the paste. Turn the mixture into a medium-sized bowl, cover, and chill for at least 2 hours.

2 Using slightly damp hands, shape the roe mixture into balls the size of walnuts. Place the flour on a plate and gently roll the balls in it to coat.

3 Heat the oil and cook the balls, in batches, for 5–8 minutes, or until crisp on the outside and cooked through. Using a slotted spoon, transfer to a dish lined with absorbent kitchen paper to drain. Serve warm or cold with lemon wedges.

Red Mullet with Garlic
BARBOUNI ME SKORTHO

◆ ◆ ◆ ◆

The tiny red mullet are best suited for the Meze table, but if they are not available, use a large one and cut it up at the table.

Preparation time: about 10 minutes
Cooking time: about 5–10 minutes
SERVES: 6

- 6 tbsp very finely chopped fresh parsley
- 6 garlic cloves, crushed
- salt and freshly ground black pepper, to taste
- 6 small red mullet, cleaned
- flour, for coating
- olive oil, for shallow frying
- chopped fresh parsley, to garnish
- lemon wedges to serve

1 In a small bowl, combine the parsley with the garlic and season with salt and freshly ground black pepper. Place about 1 tsp of the garlic mixture into the cavity of each fish and rub any remaining mixture evenly over the skins. Coat the fish lightly and evenly with the flour.

2 Heat the oil in a deep frying pan and cook the fish, no more than two at a time, for about 5–7 minutes, or until crisp on the outside and cooked through. Using a slotted spoon, transfer to a dish lined with absorbent kitchen paper to drain. Sprinkle with parsley and serve with lemon wedges.

Fish and Vegetable Casserole
PSARI YIAHNI ME LAHANO
◆ ◆ ◆ ◆

Cod, haddock or monkfish would all be suitable types of fish to use for this dish, which originates from the Greek island of Corfu. The crucial ingredient is the garlic, and plenty of it.

Preparation time: about 15 minutes
Cooking time: about 40 minutes
SERVES: 8–10

- *85 ml/3 fl oz olive oil*
- *1 large onion, sliced*
- *900 g/2 lb small new potatoes, washed and cut into 1 cm/½ in rounds*
- *2 carrots, cut into 2.5 cm/1 in chunks*
- *1 celery stick, chopped*
- *salt and freshly ground black pepper, to taste*
- *6 garlic cloves, crushed*
- *1.1 kg/2½ lb firm white fish fillets, skinned and cut into 5 cm/2 in chunks*
- *50 ml/2 fl oz freshly squeezed lemon juice*

1 Heat 50 ml/2 fl oz of the olive oil in a large, heavy-based saucepan and sauté the onion for about 3 minutes, or until softened.

2 Add the potatoes, carrots and celery, and season with salt and freshly ground black pepper. Continue to cook for a further 4–5 minutes, or until the vegetables begin to soften.

3 Stir in the garlic and pour over enough boiling water to just cover the vegetables. Bring to the boil, cover, and simmer for 10–15 minutes or until the vegetables are almost tender.

4 Gently stir the fish into the casserole, cover and simmer for 10–15 minutes or until the fish flakes easily, adding a little extra water if necessary. Just before the end of the cooking time, remove the cover and stir in the lemon juice and the remaining olive oil. Adjust the seasoning if necessary and serve.

Stuffed Fish Fillets with Egg and Lemon Sauce

FETES PSARI GEMISTES AVGOLEMONO

❖ ❖ ❖ ❖

This is most certainly a dish for a special occasion. It takes a little longer to prepare than most, but it's well worth the effort for the delicious taste and excellent presentation.

Preparation time: about 45 minutes
Cooking time: about 40 minutes
Oven temperature: 180°C/350°F/Gas 4

SERVES: 6–8

- *75 g/3 oz butter*
- *2 garlic cloves, crushed*
- *1 onion, very finely chopped*
- *½ green pepper, seeded and very finely chopped*
- *175 g/6 oz cooked, shelled prawns, roughly chopped*
- *50 g/2 oz fresh white breadcrumbs*
- *1 tbsp chopped fresh parsley*
- *salt and freshly ground black pepper, to taste*
- *4 flounder or sole fillets, skinned*
- *3 eggs*
- *6 tbsp freshly squeezed lemon juice*
- *300 ml/½ pt warm fish stock*
- *chopped fresh parsley, to garnish*

BELOW
Fish in all colours of the rainbow, on Heraklion harbour.

1 Preheat the oven to 180°C/350°F/Gas 4. Melt 25 g/1 oz of the butter in a large frying pan and sauté the garlic, onion and green pepper for about 5 minutes or until the onion is golden.

2 Add the prawns to the onion mixture with the breadcrumbs, parsley, salt and freshly ground black pepper and stir. Cook for a further minute, then remove from the heat. Cool slightly.

3 Divide the prawn mixture between the fish fillets and spread evenly. Roll up the fillets and arrange them seam-side down in a large, buttered ovenproof dish. Melt the remaining butter in a small saucepan and use to brush over the rolled fish fillets. Bake for 25–30 minutes, or until the fish flakes easily and is cooked through. Cut the rolls into 1 cm/½ in rounds and arrange on a warm serving platter. Tent with kitchen foil to keep warm.

4 To make the egg and lemon sauce: beat the eggs in a medium-sized bowl and whisk in the lemon juice, a little at a time. Very slowly whisk in the warm fish stock. Pour the sauce into a small saucepan and gently heat, whisking continuously, until slightly thickened. Pour over the fillets and sprinkle with a garnish of chopped parsley to serve.

Salt Cod Fritters with Garlic
BAKALIAROS SKORTHALIA

◆ ◆ ◆ ◆

Salt cod is generally available from delicatessens. Remember to start this recipe a day in advance as the salt cod needs soaking for 24 hours.

Preparation time: about 1 hour 30 minutes plus soaking
Cooking time: about 5–10 minutes

SERVES: 6–8

- *700 g/1½ lb salt cod, soaked in cold water for 24 hours, with frequent changes of water*
- *100 g/4 oz plain flour*
- *salt and freshly ground black pepper, to taste*
- *1 tbsp olive oil*
- *150 ml/¼ pt warm water*
- *1 egg white*
- *olive oil, for deep frying*
- *lemon wedges, to serve*

FOR THE *SKORTHALIA*
- *4 slices white bread, crusts removed*
- *6 garlic cloves, crushed*
- *salt, to taste*
- *50 g/2 oz ground almonds*
- *150 ml/¼ pt olive oil*
- *freshly squeezed juice of 1 lemon*

BELOW
The ancient city of Epidaurus is renowned for its beautiful temple of Asclepius (fourth century BC) and its theatre, pictured here.

1 To make the *Skorthalia,* place the bread in a food processor or blender and blend into fine crumbs. Sprinkle in 4 tbsp cold water and leave to soak for about 5 minutes. Add the garlic, salt and ground almonds and process until smooth and well combined.

2 With the motor still running, gradually add the olive oil in a continuous stream, until the mixture is thick and smooth. Gradually add the lemon juice in the same way. Turn into a serving bowl, cover and set aside.

3 Strip the skin and bones away from the salt cod and discard. Cut the flesh into 5 cm/2 in chunks. To make the batter for the fish; sift the flour into a large mixing bowl with the salt and freshly ground black pepper. Drizzle the olive oil over the flour and whisk in the warm water to make a smooth mixture. Allow to stand at room temperature for about 1 hour.

4 Beat the egg white in a clean, dry bowl until it holds stiff peaks, then fold into the batter. Heat the oil. Dip the chunks of fish into the batter, then gently place in the hot oil. Cook the fish in batches for about 5–7 minutes or until crisp and golden. Using a slotted spoon, transfer the cooked fritters to a dish lined with absorbent kitchen paper to drain. Serve the battered fritters with lemon wedges and the *Skorthalia.*

Summer Fish Menu

Tuna Fish with Chickpeas
Tonos me Revithia

◆

Cod's Roe Dip
Taramosalata

◆

Sesame Bread Rings
Semit

◆

Swordfish Kebabs
Xifias Souvlakia

◆

Red Mullet with Garlic
Barbouni me Skortho

◆

Greek Meze Mushrooms
Manitaria

◆

Black-eye Beans with Greens
Louvia me Lahana

◆

Meatless Stuffed Vegetables
Yemista Orphana

◆

Filo Custard Pie
Galatoboureko

◆

Marmalade Crêpes
Krep me Marmalada

◆

Wine: Retsina
(Crisp dry white)

Deep-fried Mussels
MITHIA TIGANITA

◆ ◆ ◆ ◆

In Greece, fresh mussels are abundant and cheap. However, the shelled, frozen, cooked variety may be more readily available to you, in which case all you need to do is to thaw them out before using them.

Preparation time: about 30 minutes
Cooking time: about 15–20 minutes
SERVES: 6–8

- 900 g/2 lb fresh mussels
- vegetable oil, for deep frying
- lemon wedges, to serve

FOR THE BATTER
- 2 eggs
- 50 g/2 oz plain flour
- salt and freshly ground black pepper, to taste
- 2 tbsp chopped fresh parsley
- ½ tsp ground cinnamon

1 Wash and scrub the mussels under cold running water, removing the 'beards' and discarding any mussels that are even partially opened. Place the prepared mussels in a large saucepan.

2 Cover the mussels with water and bring to the boil. Cook for about 10 minutes, or until the shells have opened and the mussels are cooked. Drain, discarding any which have not opened. Allow the mussels to cool slightly, then remove them from their shells.

3 To make the batter, place the eggs in a medium-sized mixing bowl and beat until frothy. Sift in the flour and beat until smooth. Add 4 tbsp cold water and season with salt and freshly ground black pepper. Stir in the chopped parsley and ground cinnamon.

4 Heat the oil. Dip the mussels, one at a time, in the batter then carefully place in the hot oil. Cook the mussels in batches for a few seconds, or until crisp on the outside. Using a slotted spoon, transfer to a dish lined with absorbent kitchen paper to drain. Serve the mussels warm with lemon wedges.

Swordfish Kebabs
XIFIAS SOUVLAKIA

◆ ◆ ◆ ◆

Swordfish is ideal for this recipe because it is a firm-fleshed fish with plenty of taste, so the kebabs stay intact during cooking and the result is delicious.

Preparation time: about 15 minutes plus marinating
Cooking time: about 15–20 minutes
SERVES: 6–8

- 120 ml/4 fl oz olive oil
- freshly squeezed juice of 2 lemons
- 2 tsp dried oregano
- salt and freshly ground black pepper, to taste
- 900 g/2 lb fresh
- swordfish, skinned, filleted and cut into 5 cm/2 in chunks
- 4 tomatoes, quartered
- 2 green peppers, seeded and cut into large chunks
- 3 onions, quartered

1 In a small bowl, combine the olive oil, lemon juice, oregano, salt and freshly ground black pepper. Place the swordfish in a large, shallow dish. Pour the olive oil mixture over the fish, cover, and marinate for 2 hours.

2 Reserve the marinade, and divide the swordfish cubes, tomato wedges, chunks of green pepper and onion quarters evenly between six or eight metal skewers. Lay the kebabs on a grill rack.

3 Preheat the grill and cook the kebabs for 10–15 minutes or until the fish flakes easily and the vegetables are tender, basting frequently with the reserved marinade and turning the kebabs during cooking. Serve immediately.

Small Fish in Vine Leaves

PSARI STA KLIMATOFILLA

◆ ◆ ◆ ◆

Vine leaves are perfect for wrapping around small, oily fish to hold in the flavours and to prevent the fish from falling apart during cooking. This is an attractive and unusual Greek speciality which works successfully on the barbecue.

Preparation time: about 30 minutes
Cooking time: about 10–15 minutes
SERVES: 6

- 6 small mackerel or herring, scaled and cleaned
- freshly squeezed juice of 1 lemon
- salt and freshly ground black pepper, to taste
- olive oil, to drizzle
- 3 tsp dried thyme or 4 tsp fresh thyme
- 12 vine leaves, boiled for 5 minutes, drained and rinsed
- fresh thyme sprigs, to garnish
- lemon wedges, to serve

1 Wash the fish under cold running water and pat dry with absorbent kitchen paper. Place the fish on a chopping board and sprinkle the lemon juice over it. Season with salt and freshly ground black pepper.

2 Drizzle the fish evenly with some olive oil and sprinkle the thyme over it. Lay the vine leaves out on the work surface and lightly brush with a little olive oil. Use two of the vine leaves to wrap around each fish, completely encasing it.

3 Arrange the wrapped fish on a lighly oiled grill rack and cook under a preheated grill for about 6 minutes, on each side, or until the fish flakes easily and is cooked through. Transfer to a serving platter and garnish with fresh thyme sprigs. Serve with plenty of lemon wedges.

Prawn Pilaf

PILAFI ME GARIDES

◆ ◆ ◆ ◆

Try this recipe using cooked shelled mussels instead of the prawns – it makes a delicious variation.

Preparation time: about 20 minutes
Cooking time: about 25 minutes
SERVES: 6 – 8

- 4 tbsp olive oil
- 2 garlic cloves, crushed
- 1 large onion, sliced
- 2 celery sticks, chopped
- 100 g/4 oz long-grain rice
- 400 g/14 oz can chopped tomatoes
- 2 tsp dried majoram
- salt and freshly ground black pepper, to taste
- 150 ml/¼ pt hot fish stock
- 1 tsp sugar
- 2 tsp lemon juice
- 350 g/12 oz large cooked shelled prawns
- 100 g/4 oz feta cheese, crumbled
- chopped fresh parsley, to garnish

1 Heat the oil in a large frying pan and sauté the garlic, onion and celery for about 5 minutes or until softened. Stir in the rice and continue to cook for a further minute.

2 Add the chopped tomatoes and majoram and season with salt and freshly ground black pepper. Add the fish stock, sugar and lemon juice and bring the mixture to the boil. Cover and simmer for 10–15 minutes or until the rice is tender, stirring occasionally.

3 Stir in the prawns and cook for a further 3–5 minutes. Sprinkle over the cheese and gently stir to incorporate. Remove from the heat and keep covered for a final 1–2 minutes, or until the cheese just melts. Sprinkle with chopped fresh parsley and serve from the pan.

Sardines Cooked with Tomatoes and Rosemary

SARTHELA MARINATA

◆ ◆ ◆ ◆

It has been said that once you have tasted this classic Greek dish, you'll dream of Greece forever.

Preparation time: about 30 minutes
Cooking time: about 35 minutes
SERVES: 8

- 8 fresh sardines, cleaned, heads removed
- flour, for coating
- olive oil, for shallow frying

FOR THE SAUCE
- 50 ml/2 fl oz olive oil
- 1 tbsp plain flour
- 50 ml/2 fl oz red wine vinegar
- 400 g/14 oz can chopped tomatoes
- 2 tsp dried rosemary, or 3 tsp chopped fresh rosemary
- 1 tsp dried oregano
- 2 garlic cloves, crushed
- salt and freshly ground black pepper, to taste
- 1 tsp sugar
- fresh rosemary sprigs, to garnish
- lemon wedges, to serve

1 Wash the sardines and pat dry with absorbent kitchen paper. Lay out on a chopping board and dredge with flour on both sides.

2 Heat the oil and cook the fish, in batches, for about 5 minutes, or until golden and cooked through. Using a slotted spoon, transfer the fish to a dish lined with absorbent kitchen paper to drain. Tent the fish with kitchen foil to keep warm.

3 To make the sauce; heat the olive oil in a medium-sized saucepan and stir in the flour to make a paste. Cook for 30 seconds, then gradually stir in the red wine vinegar and add the chopped tomatoes, rosemary, oregano and garlic. Season with salt and freshly ground black pepper and stir in the sugar. Cover and simmer for 15–20 minutes, until thickened, stirring occasionally.

4 Arrange the sardines on a warm serving platter and pour the sauce over them. Garnish with fresh rosemary sprigs and serve with lemon wedges.

Buffet Party Menu

Greek Potato Salad
Patatosalata

◆

Roast Pepper Salad
Piperies Orektiko

◆

Marinated Meatballs
Keftedakia me Saltsa

◆

Garlic Roast Potatoes
Patates me Skortho

◆

Stuffed Vine Leaves
Dolmades

◆

Moussaka

◆

Lamb Kebabs
Souvlakia

◆

Fried Chicken Balls
Koto Tighanito

◆

Salt Cod Fritters with Garlic
Bakaliaros Skorthalia

◆

Nut-Stuffed Lady's Fingers
Dkaktyla

◆

Sweet Cheese Pastries
Kaltsounia Cretis

◆

Sweet Meze

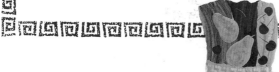

Marmalade Crêpes

KREP ME MARMELADA

The crêpes can be made far in advance and stacked on a plate. Cover with kitchen foil and reheat in a low oven for about 15 minutes before finishing with the marmalade and cinnamon sugar to serve.

Preparation time: about 30 minutes
Cooking time: about 15 minutes
MAKES: ABOUT 24

- 2 eggs, beaten
- 1 tbsp caster sugar
- few drops of vanilla essence
- 600 ml/1 pt milk
- 225 g/8 oz plain flour, sifted
- butter, for greasing
- marmalade, to serve
- ground cinnamon mixed with caster sugar, to serve

1 Place the eggs and sugar in a medium-sized bowl and whisk, preferably with an electric mixer, until thick, pale and frothy. Whisk in the vanilla essence and then the milk, a little at a time, until well combined.

2 Whisk the sifted flour into the egg mixture, a little at a time, whisking well after each addition to prevent any lumps from forming.

3 Melt a little butter in a small crêpe pan or frying pan and add about 2 tbsp of the batter, swirling it around to cover the base of the pan evenly. Cook over high heat for a few seconds, or until golden underneath, then flip over with a spatula and cook for a further few seconds until golden.

4 Tip the cooked crêpe on to a plate and continue with the remaining batter, melting a little extra butter in the pan if necessary. Pile up the cooked crêpes, interleaving them with sheets of greaseproof paper to prevent them sticking together.

5 To serve, spread a little marmalade over each crêpe and roll up thinly. Arrange the rolled crêpes on a warm serving plate, overlapping and piling them up where necessary. Sprinkle with the cinnamon sugar mixture while still warm.

Nut-stuffed Lady's Fingers
THAKTYLA KYPRIAKA

◆ ◆ ◆ ◆

Crisp pastry, covered in a sweet syrup and filled with a delicious nutty centre – be sure to make plenty as your guests will keep coming back for more. Rose water is available from good health food shops and delicatessens.

Preparation time: about 1 hour plus resting
Cooking time: about 5–10 minutes
MAKES: ABOUT 30–40

- *vegetable oil, for deep-fat frying*
- *175 g/6 oz pistachio nuts, shelled and roughly chopped*
- *1 tsp ground cinnamon*

FOR THE SYRUP
- *450 g/1 lb caster sugar*
- *50 ml/2 fl oz clear honey*
- *375 ml/12 fl oz water*
- *strip of lemon zest*
- *2 tbsp rose water (optional)*
- *2 tbsp freshly squeezed lemon juice*

FOR THE DOUGH
- *550 g/1¼ lb plain flour plus extra for dredging*
- *¼ tsp salt*
- *50 g/2 oz butter*
- *25 g/1 oz vegetable lard*
- *2 tbsp water*
- *1 egg yolk*

FOR THE FILLING
- *1 egg white*
- *25 g/1 oz caster sugar*
- *225 g/8 oz ground almonds*
- *2 tsp ground cinnamon*

1 To make the syrup; place the sugar and honey in a medium-sized saucepan and stir in the water. Bring to the boil over gentle heat and add the lemon zest and rose water, if using. Simmer for about 5 minutes, then remove from the heat. Stir in the lemon juice and set aside to cool, uncovered.

2 To make the dough; sift the flour and salt together in a large mixing bowl and make a well in the centre. Add the butter and vegetable lard and rub into the flour until the mixture resembles fine breadcrumbs. Stir in the water and egg yolk and mix to form a stiff dough. Turn out on to a lightly floured work surface and knead the dough until smooth. Place in a plastic bag and set aside to rest for about 1 hour.

3 To make the filling; place the egg white in a clean, dry medium-sized bowl and add the sugar. Whisk until the mixture holds stiff peaks, then fold in the ground almonds and ground cinnamon.

4 Roll out the dough on a large, clean, lightly floured work surface until it is very thin, almost translucent. Cut the dough into 5 × 10 cm/2 × 4 in rectangles. Place about ½ tsp of the filling mixture at one of the short ends of each pastry rectangle and roll up to form a finger shape. Using a fork dipped in cold water, press the two ends of each finger to seal in the filling, stretching it slightly at the same time.

5 Heat the oil in a deep-fat fryer and cook the pastry fingers in batches, for 3–5 minutes or until crisp and golden. Using a slotted spoon, transfer to a dish lined with absorbent kitchen paper to drain.

6 Mix together the chopped pistachios and the ground cinnamon in a small bowl and spread out on a plate. Dip the hot pastry fingers into the cooled syrup, then roll immediately in the chopped nuts mixture. Arrange on a serving plate and serve warm or cold.

Chocolate Refrigerator Torte
TOURTA TSOKOLATAS PSIGIOU

◆ ◆ ◆ ◆

Tourta Tsokolatas Psigiou is a deliciously rich chocolate dessert which can be made several days in advance.

Preparation time: about 20 minutes plus freezing
Cooking time: none
SERVES: 10−12

- 225 g/8 oz rich-tea biscuits, roughly broken
- 120 ml/4 fl oz milk
- 2 tbsp brandy
- 225 g/8 oz butter, softened
- 225 g/8 oz caster sugar
- 3 eggs, separated
- 2 tsp vanilla essence
- 4 tbsp cocoa powder
- 100 g/4 oz blanched almonds, toasted and roughly chopped
- vegetable oil, for greasing

1 Place the biscuits in a large mixing bowl. Pour the milk and brandy over them and allow to soak until the liquid has been absorbed.

2 Place the butter and sugar in a medium-sized bowl and beat until well blended and creamy. Beat in the egg yolks, then add the vanilla essence, cocoa powder and chopped nuts.

3 Whisk the egg whites in a clean, dry bowl and fold into the chocolate mixture. Stir in the soaked biscuits. Lightly grease a 1.2 l/2 pt loaf tin, line with greaseproof paper and pour in the biscuit mixture. Spread evenly in the dish and freeze for about 4 hours, or until solid. Remove from the freezer about 30 minutes before serving and keep chilled in the refrigerator. Turn out on to a serving plate and cut into thin slices to serve.

Coconut Syrup Cake
PASTA A LA POLITA
◆ ◆ ◆ ◆

A light, golden sponge, soaked in syrup to give it an irresistible texture. The cake can be kept in an air-tight container for at least two weeks.

Preparation time: about 1 hour
Cooking time: about 40 minutes
Oven temperature: 190°C/375°F/Gas 5
SERVES: 10—12

FOR THE SYRUP
- 375 g/12 oz caster sugar
- 1 cinnamon stick
- 1 tbsp brandy

FOR THE CAKE
- 225 g/8 oz butter, softened, plus extra for greasing

- 375 g/12 oz caster sugar
- 6 eggs, separated
- 1 tbsp brandy
- 1 tbsp freshly squeezed orange juice
- 450 g/1 lb flour
- 1 tbsp baking powder
- 175 g/6 oz desiccated coconut

1 To make the syrup; place the water in a medium-sized saucepan. Add the sugar and heat gently, stirring occasionally, until all the sugar has dissolved. Add the cinnamon stick and brandy and bring to the boil. Boil for about 5 minutes, then remove from the heat and allow to cool down.

2 Preheat the oven to 190°C/375°F/Gas 5. Grease a 23 × 30 × 7.5 cm/9 × 12 × 3 in roasting tin with butter and line with greaseproof paper. To make the cake; place the butter and sugar in a mixing bowl and beat until fluffy. Add the egg yolks, one at a time, beating well after each addition. Beat in the brandy and orange juice.

3 Sift together the flour and baking powder and gradually beat into the creamed mixture. Finally beat in the desiccated coconut. Whisk the egg whites in a clean, dry bowl until they hold stiff peaks. Fold into the creamed mixture, then pour into the prepared tin. Bake for 30–35 minutes or until golden brown and an inserted skewer comes out clean.

4 Place the cake, still in its tin, on a wire rack. Score the cake with a sharp knife to make diamond-shaped pieces. Pour the cooled syrup evenly over the cake and allow to stand for at least 15 minutes before fully cutting into pieces for serving or transferring to an air-tight container.

Almond Cakes

A M Y G T H A L O T A

Rose and orange waters are available from good health food shops and delicatessens. Ground almonds can be used and the mixing may be done by hand instead of using a food processor.

Preparation time: about 20 minutes
Cooking time: about 15 minutes
Oven temperature: 180°C/350°F/Gas 4
MAKES: ABOUT 24

- 450 g/1 lb blanched almonds
- 225 g/8 oz caster sugar
- 1 tsp vanilla essence
- 3 egg whites
- 150 g/5 oz fresh white breadcrumbs
- butter, for greasing
- 300 ml/½ pt orange or rose water
- caster sugar, for dredging

1 Preheat the oven to 180°C/350°F/Gas 4. Place the almonds and 2 tbsp of the sugar in a food processor and blend until very fine. Add the remaining sugar with the vanilla essence. Lightly beat the egg whites in a clean bowl and add to the food processor with the bread-crumbs. Blend until a soft dough is formed, then turn the mixture out on to the work surface.

2 Lighly butter two baking sheets. Using slightly damp hands, shape the almond mixture into walnut-sized balls and arrange on the prepared baking sheets. Bake for about 15 minutes or until golden and firm on the outside.

3 Allow the cakes to cool slightly, then transfer them to a wire rack. Pour the orange or rose water into a small bowl and dip each cake into the liquid, then return to the wire rack. Dredge with caster sugar and allow to dry before serving.

Nut Pastries

BAKLAVA

A mixture of walnuts and almonds is used in this version of the classic Greek pastry, but if you prefer you can stick to one or the other – or indeed, try using pistachios instead.

Preparation time: about 45 minutes
Cooking time: about 1 hour 15 minutes
Oven temperature: 160°C/325°F/Gas 3

MAKES: ABOUT 24

- 175 g/6 oz unsalted butter, melted
- 450 g/1 lb filo pastry, thawed if frozen

FOR THE FILLING
- 4 tbsp clear honey
- 2 tbsp freshly squeezed lemon juice
- 50 g/2 oz caster sugar
- 2 tsp ground cinnamon
- 1 tsp finely grated lemon zest

- 225 g/8 oz blanched almonds, roughly chopped
- 225 g/8 oz shelled walnuts, roughly chopped

FOR THE SYRUP
- 350 g/12 oz caster sugar
- 100 g/4 oz clear honey
- 600 ml/1 pt water
- 1 cinnamon stick
- strip of lemon rind

1 Preheat the oven to 160°C/325°F/Gas 3. Butter a 30 × 23 × 7.5 cm/12 × 9 × 3 in roasting tin. Trim the sheets of filo pastry to fit inside the tin and discard the trimmings.

2 Place the first sheet of filo pastry in the base of the prepared tin and brush evenly with melted butter. Lay another sheet of filo pastry on top and brush again with the melted butter. Repeat this process until you have 12 sheets of filo pastry layered on the bottom of the tin. Cover the remaining filo pastry with a slightly damp cloth to prevent it from drying out while you work.

3 To make the filling; place the honey in a medium-sized bowl. Add the lemon juice and stir until combined. Stir in the sugar, ground cinnamon, lemon zest and nuts. Spread half of the filling mixture over the pastry in the base of the tin.

4 Layer another three sheets of filo pastry on top of the filling, brushing each sheet with melted butter. Spread the remaining filling mixture over the pastry and cover with the remaining sheets of filo pastry, brushing each sheet with melted butter. Brush the top with any remaining butter and score into 5 cm/2 in diamond shapes. Bake for about 1 hour, or until crisp and golden. Remove from the oven and stand on a wire rack.

5 To make the syrup; place all the ingredients together in a medium-sized saucepan and heat gently until the sugar has dissolved completely. Increase the heat and boil rapidly for about 10 minutes, without stirring. Set aside to cool. Discard the cinnamon stick and lemon rind and pour the syrup evenly over the pastry. Ideally, the *Baklava* should stand at room temperature overnight before it is cut into diamond-shaped pieces.

Filo Custard Pie
GALAKTOBOUREKO

◆ ◆ ◆ ◆

Another Greek classic – a similar idea to *Baklava* and just as sweet and irresistible.

Preparation time: about 1 hour
Cooking time: about 1 hour 30 minutes
Oven temperature: 180°C/350°F/Gas 5
MAKES: ABOUT 24

- 450 g/1 lb filo pastry
- 100 g/4 oz unsalted butter, melted

- 2 tsp freshly squeezed lemon juice

FOR THE SYRUP
- 450 g/1 lb caster sugar
- 300 ml/½ pt water
- 1 cinnamon stick
- few whole cloves
- 1 tbsp brandy
- 1 tbsp freshly squeezed orange juice

FOR THE FILLING
- 225 g/8 oz caster sugar
- 225 g/8 oz fine semolina
- 1.4 l/2½ pt milk
- 1 tbsp brandy
- 3 eggs
- finely grated zest of ½ orange

1 To make the syrup; place the sugar and water in a large saucepan and stir over a low heat until all the sugar has dissolved. Add the cinnamon stick and cloves and bring to the boil. Boil rapidly for 10–12 minutes. Remove from the heat and stir in the remaining syrup ingredients. Set aside to cool. Remove and discard the cinnamon stick and whole cloves.

2 Preheat the oven at 180°C/350°F/Gas 5. Lightly butter a 30 × 23 × 7.5 cm/12 × 9 × 3 in roasting tin.

3 To make the filling; place the sugar and semolina in a large saucepan. Gradually stir in the milk and heat gently, stirring continuously, until the mixture thickens, making sure no lumps appear. Stir in the brandy and remove from the heat.

4 Place the eggs in a mixing bowl and whisk until pale and frothy. Add the semolina mixture and whisk again until evenly combined. Add the orange zest. Allow to cool down slightly.

5 Layer about half of the filo pastry in the base of the prepared tin, brushing each sheet evenly with melted butter before layering the next. Spoon in the filling mixture and spread evenly over the base. Top with the remaining sheets of filo pastry, brushing each one with the melted butter.

6 Using a sharp knife, score the top layers of filo pastry, dividing the pie into 5 cm/2 in diamonds or squares. Bake for about 45 minutes, or until crisp and golden on top and the filling is set. Remove from the oven and stand the tin on a wire rack. Pour the syrup evenly over the top of the *Galaktoboureko* and leave to stand for at least 4 hours, but preferably overnight. Serve cut into small pieces.

Honey Turnovers
DIPLES

◆ ◆ ◆ ◆

A favourite tea-time treat in Greece; thin pieces of dough are fried in hot oil, then coated in a honey syrup, chopped walnuts and cinnamon.

Preparation time: about 30 minutes
Cooking time: about 20 minutes
MAKES: ABOUT 60

- *3 eggs, plus 3 egg yolks*
- *2 tbsp freshly squeezed orange juice*
- *2 tsp baking powder*
- *800 g/1¾ lb plain flour*
- *vegetable oil, for deep frying*

FOR THE SYRUP
- *450 g/1 lb jar clear honey*
- *120 ml/4 fl oz water*
- *2 tsp ground cinnamon*
- *275 g/10 oz shelled walnuts, chopped*

1 Place the eggs and extra yolks in a mixing bowl and beat well. Beat in the orange juice. Sift the baking powder together with 450 g/1 lb of the flour and beat into the egg mixture. Add enough of the remaining flour to make a stiff dough.

2 Turn the dough out on to a lightly floured surface and lightly knead for about 10 minutes, or until bubbles and blisters begin to appear.

3 Cut the dough into four equal parts and roll out each quarter on the floured work surface until paper thin. Cut the dough into 10 × 15 cm/4 × 6 in rectangles and set aside. Heat the oil and fry the strips, a few at a time, for a few seconds, or until golden brown and crisp, turning them over during cooking with the use of two forks. Using a slotted spoon, transfer to a dish lined with absorbent kitchen paper to drain.

4 To make the syrup; place the honey and water in a large saucepan and heat gently until the honey has melted. Bring to the boil and cook for about 15 minutes, skimming any froth from the top as the syrup boils. Remove from the heat. Dip each turnover into the hot syrup and place on a wire rack to cool. Sprinkle over the ground cinnamon and chopped walnuts and allow to cool before serving.

Christmas Shortbread

K O U R A B I E T H E S

◆ ◆ ◆ ◆

These are found piled high in the cake shops all over Greece just before Christmas. Make plenty in advance and store in an airtight container, ready to celebrate the season's festivities.

Preparation time: about 20 minutes
Cooking time: about 20 minutes
Oven temperature: 190°C/375°F/Gas 5
MAKES: ABOUT 26

- 450 g/1 lb unsalted butter, softened
- 225 g/8 oz caster sugar
- 3 egg yolks
- 4 tbsp brandy
- few drops of vanilla essence
- 900 g/2 lb self-raising flour, sifted
- 225 g/8 oz blanched almonds, toasted and chopped
- 4 tbsp rose water
- icing sugar, sifted, to dredge

1 Preheat the oven to 190°C/375°F/Gas 5. Place the butter and sugar in a mixing bowl and cream together until light and fluffy. Beat in the egg yolks, then the brandy and the vanilla essence.

2 Sift in the flour and add the almonds. Mix well to form a stiff dough. Turn out on to a lightly floured surface and gently knead the dough for a few seconds.

3 Roll out to 5 mm/¼ in thick and cut into shapes using pastry cutters in the shapes of stars, half moons and circles. Place the dough shapes on lightly buttered baking sheets and cook for about 20 minutes or until the biscuits are firm but not coloured.

4 Transfer to a wire rack to cool, then sprinkle with the rose water. Allow to dry, then dredge heavily with icing sugar. Pile on to a plate to serve.

Honey Doughnuts
L O U K O U M A D E S
◆ ◆ ◆ ◆

A Greek speciality – served with strong black coffee to complement the sweet, moist, nutty flavour of these delectable morsels.

Preparation time: about 30 minutes
Cooking time: about 5–10 minutes
MAKES: ABOUT 30

- 300 ml/½ pt water
- 20 g/¾ oz fresh yeast
- 350 g/12 oz flour
- ½ tsp ground cinnamon
- small pinch of salt
- 6 tbsp warm milk
- 2 eggs, beaten
- vegetable oil, for deep-fat frying
- 50 g/2 oz caster sugar
- 1 tsp ground cinnamon
- 100 g/4 oz blanched almonds, toasted and finely chopped

FOR THE SYRUP
- 225 g/8 oz clear honey
- 100 g/4 oz caster sugar
- 1 tbsp lemon juice
- 1 cinnamon stick

1 Place 150 ml/¼ pt lukewarm water in a small bowl and sprinkle the yeast over it. Stir well until all the yeast has dissolved, cover, and set aside in a warm place for 15–20 minutes or until the mixture is frothy.

2 Sift the flour with the cinnamon and salt into a mixing bowl and make a well in the centre. Pour in the frothy yeast mixture, the milk and the remaining 150 ml/¼ pt lukewarm water. Gradually stir in the flour mixture from the sides of the bowl, then beat in the eggs to form a smooth batter. Beat the batter vigorously until bubbles appear on the surface. Set aside.

3 To make the syrup, place all the ingredients in a medium-sized saucepan and heat gently until the sugar has melted. Increase the heat and boil the syrup for about 10 minutes. Allow to cool, then remove the cinnamon stick and set aside.

4 Heat the oil for deep-fat frying. Carefully place the batter, 1 tbsp at a time, into the hot oil and fry the doughnuts in batches for 3–5 minutes or until puffed and golden brown, turning them as they cook. Continue with the remaining batter. Using a slotted spoon, transfer the cooked doughnuts to a dish lined with absorbent kitchen paper to drain.

5 Mix together the caster sugar and ground cinnamon on a plate and roll each hot doughnut in the mixture to coat. Either arrange the doughnuts in a shallow serving dish, pour over the syrup and allow to stand for about 1 hour before scattering over the chopped almonds, or pile the doughnuts on to a plate and scatter with the chopped almonds and serve the syrup separately.

Easter Biscuits
KOULOURAKIA LAMBRIATIKA
◆ ◆ ◆ ◆

These are a staple on the Greek Easter Meze table and are dunked into breakfast coffee for weeks after the end of the festivities.

Preparation time: about 30 minutes plus resting
Cooking time: about 20 minutes
Oven temperature: 180°C/350°F/Gas 4
MAKES: ABOUT 48

- 800 g/1¾ lb strong plain flour
- 1 tbsp baking powder
- pinch of salt
- 175 g/6 oz butter, softened
- 175 g/6 oz caster sugar
- 2 eggs
- 120 ml/4 fl oz milk
- finely grated zest of ½ orange
- finely grated zest of ½ lemon
- few drops of vanilla essence
- 1 egg yolk mixed with 1 tbsp freshly squeezed orange juice, to glaze
- sesame seeds, to decorate

1 Preheat the oven to 180°C/350°F/Gas 4. Sift together the flour, baking powder and pinch of salt in a medium-sized bowl.

2 Place the butter and sugar in another mixing bowl and beat, using an electric whisk, until light and fluffy. Beat in the eggs, one at a time, then beat in the milk. Add the orange and lemon zests and the vanilla essence and beat well.

3 Gradually add the flour mixture, a little at a time, to form a thick, smooth dough. Turn out on to a lightly floured surface and gently knead the dough until soft. Allow the dough to rest for about 10 minutes.

4 Divide the dough into pieces the size of a walnut and shape into ropes, 'S' shapes, twists, rings or rounds, making sure the biscuits are all the same size, if not the same shape, to ensure even cooking.

5 Arrange the biscuits on lightly greased baking sheets and brush with the egg yolk and orange mixture to glaze. Sprinkle with sesame seeds and bake for 15–20 minutes or until golden. Transfer to a wire rack to cool.

Sweet Cheese Pastries

KALTSOUNIA CRETIS

◆ ◆ ◆ ◆

This recipe originates from the island of Crete, where *Kaltsounia Cretis* can be found fresh from the oven in bakery shops day or night. The cheese for the filling is available from good Greek delicatessens. These pastries will keep for two weeks in an airtight container in a cool, dry place.

Preparation time: about 40 minutes plus standing
Cooking time: about 25 minutes
Oven temperature: 180°C/350°F/Gas 4
MAKES: ABOUT 30

- icing sugar, sifted, to dredge

FOR THE DOUGH
- 450 g/1 lb plain flour, sifted
- 1 tsp baking powder
- 1 tbsp granulated sugar
- pinch of salt
- 50 g/2 oz butter, cubed, plus extra for greasing
- 50 g/2 oz vegetable lard, cubed
- 2 eggs
- 2 tsp orange water
- 1–2 tbsp milk

FOR THE FILLING
- 450 g/1 lb soft cheese, eg saltless mizithra, anthotiro or ricotta
- 1 egg
- 75 g/3 oz granulated sugar
- 2 tbsp clear honey
- 1 tsp ground cinnamon
- ½ tsp dried mint

BELOW
Pastry is an art form in this charming bakery in Heraklion.

1 To make the dough; sift the flour, baking powder, sugar and salt together in a large mixing bowl. Rub in the butter and vegetable lard until the mixture resembles fine breadcrumbs.

2 Mix in the eggs, orange water and milk until the dough is soft and elastic. Turn out on to a lightly floured surface and knead the dough for about 10 minutes until it is smooth and soft. Return to the cleaned bowl and set aside, covered.

3 To make the filling; combine all the ingredients together in a large bowl and mix well. Lightly grease two baking sheets with butter and preheat the oven to 180°C/350°F/Gas 4.

4 Divide the dough into walnut-sized pieces. Roll each piece out on a lightly floured surface to a 10-cm/4-in circle. Place 1 tsp of the cheese filling mixture in the centre of each circle and fold in the edges of the dough until they just meet, leaving the filling slightly exposed in the middle.

5 Place the cheese pastries on the prepared baking sheets and cook for 20–25 minutes or until lightly browned and crisp. Transfer to a wire rack to cool, then dredge with icing sugar.

Mixed Fruit Compôte

KOMPOSTA ANAMIKTI

◆ ◆ ◆ ◆

The perfect accompaniment to this delicious dessert is lashings of thick Greek yoghurt.

Preparation time: about 30 minutes
Cooking time: about 15 minutes
SERVES: 8—10

- 350 g/12 oz pears
- 350 g/12 oz apples
- 350 g/12 oz peaches
- 350 g/12 oz apricots
- 2 tbsp freshly squeezed lemon juice
- 700 g/1½ lb caster sugar
- 2 cinnamon sticks
- 900 ml/1½ pt water
- 3–4 whole cloves
- strip of lemon rind

1 Prepare the fruit for the compôte: peel, core and quarter the pears, apples. Wash the peaches and apricots, and remove the stones. Cut the peaches into quarters and apricots in half.

2 Place the pear and apple quarters in a large, heavy-based saucepan with the lemon juice, sugar, cinnamon sticks, water, cloves and lemon rind. Gently bring to the boil and simmer for 5 minutes.

3 Add the peaches and cook for a further 5 minutes, then add the apricot halves and continue to cook for 3–5 minutes or until softened. Using a slotted spoon, transfer the fruit to a serving bowl, cover and set aside.

4 Return the syrup to the boil and continue to boil rapidly for about 10 minutes, or until reduced slightly and thickened. Remove the cinnamon sticks, cloves and lemon rind. Allow the syrup to cool, then pour over the fruit. Serve at room temperature or chilled.

New Year Cake
VASSILOPITTA
◆ ◆ ◆ ◆

Vassilopitta is traditionally served on New Year's Day. Whoever is lucky enough to find the hidden coin in their serving must be careful not to bite on it!

Preparation time: about 40 minutes plus proving
Cooking time: about 50 minutes
Oven temperature: 190°C/375°F/Gas 5
SERVES: 10–12

- 1 kg/2.2 lb plain flour
- pinch of salt
- 250 ml/8 fl oz lukewarm milk
- 50 g/2 oz fresh yeast
- 4 eggs
- 100 g/4 oz caster sugar
- 225 g/8 oz unsalted butter, melted, plus extra for greasing
- milk, to glaze
- 3 tbsp toasted sesame seeds, to decorate

1 Sift the flour and salt into a large mixing bowl. Pour the lukewarm milk into a small bowl and scatter the yeast over it. Stir well until the yeast has dissolved, then cover and set aside in a warm place until frothy.

2 Make a well in the centre of the flour mixture and beat in the eggs, one at a time, beating well after each addition. Beat in the caster sugar, melted butter and the yeast mixture. Continue to mix until the dough forms a mass, then turn out on to a lightly floured surface and knead until smooth and elastic.

3 Return the dough to the cleaned mixing bowl and cover with cling wrap. Set aside in a warm place to prove for about 2 hours or until doubled in size.

4 Preheat the oven to 190°C/375°F/Gas 5. Turn the dough out on to a lightly floured surface and knead again for about 5 minutes. Press a clean coin into the dough and continue to knead for a further 1–2 minutes. Shape the dough into a round and press into a buttered 20 cm/8 in round cake tin. Cover with cling wrap and leave in a warm place to prove for a further 10 minutes.

5 Brush the top of the cake with milk and sprinkle with the toasted sesame seeds. Bake for about 50 minutes or until golden on top and hollow-sounding when tapped. Transfer to a wire rack to cool. Serve cut into slices.

Spoon Sweets
GLIKA KOUTALIOU
◆ ◆ ◆ ◆

Make jars of these tempting sweets when the fruits are in season, as they keep for several months stored in a cool, dry place. The Greeks would serve these sweets to visitors, with a cup of coffee and a glass of iced water. Spoon a few pieces of fruit with a little of the syrup out on to small dishes for guests to help themselves.

Preparation time: about 30 minutes plus standing
Cooking time: about 20 minutes
MAKES: ABOUT 3 × 450 G/1 LB JARS

- 1 kg/2¼ lb fresh fruit, including cherries, gooseberries, grapes, figs
- 600 ml/1 pt water
- 700 g/1½ lb caster sugar
- 2 tbsp freshly squeezed lemon juice
- strip of lemon zest
- few drops of vanilla essence

1 Prepare the fruit: stone the cherries, top and tail the gooseberries, seed the grapes and so on.

2 Pour the water into a large saucepan and add the sugar. Heat gently until the sugar has dissolved, stirring continuously. Increase the heat and boil the syrup, without stirring, for 5 minutes.

3 Add the fruit to the syrup with the lemon zest and vanilla essence and simmer for 10 minutes. Pour the mixture into a heatproof bowl, cover, and leave overnight in a cool place.

4 Return the fruit in the syrup to the cleaned saucepan and bring to the boil again. Simmer for 5 minutes, then pour back into the bowl. Cover and leave overnight once again.

5 Remove and discard the lemon zest. Spoon the fruit and syrup into warm, sterilized screw-top jars. Cool, label and store until required.

Breads to Serve
with Meze

Classic Olive Bread

Pitta Bread

Sesame Bread Rings

Sesame Rolls

Christmas Bread

Easter Bread

Classic Olive Bread

E L I O P I T T A

◆ ◆ ◆ ◆

The olives in this bread are sometimes added unpitted. For an extra-luxurious finish, brush the bread with some beaten egg yolk 15 minutes before the end of the cooking time.

Preparation time: about 30 minutes plus resting
Cooking time: about 50 minutes
Oven temperature: 190°C/375°F/Gas 5
MAKES: 1 LOAF

- 800 g/1¾ lb strong plain flour
- 1 tbsp baking powder
- pinch of salt
- 175 ml/6 fl oz water
- 50 ml/2 fl oz olive oil plus extra for greasing
- 1 tbsp dried mint
- 1 onion, finely chopped
- 375 g/12 oz olives, pitted, rinsed and dried
- 1 egg yolk, beaten, to glaze

1 Preheat the oven to 190°C/375°F/Gas 5. Sift the flour, baking powder and salt together in a large mixing bowl and make a well in the centre.

2 Pour the water into the well with the olive oil, dried mint, chopped onion and the olives. Stir well with a wooden spoon to form a stiff dough. Tun the mixture out on to a lightly floured work surface and knead the dough for at least 10 minutes until smooth and soft. Return to the cleaned bowl, cover with cling wrap and leave to rest for about 10 minutes.

3 Turn the dough out once more on to a lightly floured work surface. Knead and shape into a 24-cm/9½-in round. Lightly oil a 25-cm/10-in pie dish and place the dough in it. Bake for about 50 minutes, brushing the surface of the bread with the beaten egg yolk 15 minutes before the end of the cooking time. Transfer the bread to a wire rack to cool before serving.

Pitta Bread

PITTA

❖ ❖ ❖ ❖

There's nothing quite like the taste of freshly baked pitta bread, served with an array of tempting dishes at the Meze table. Pitta bread freezes well, too. You can thaw it out and warm it up by putting it in a moderate oven for just a few minutes before serving.

Preparation time: about 30 minutes plus proving
Cooking time: about 10 minutes
Oven temperature: 240°C/475°F/Gas 9

MAKES: ABOUT 12

- 6 tsp dried yeast
- 1 tsp caster sugar
- 600 ml/1 pt warm water
- 1.4 kg/3 lb strong plain
- *flour, plus extra for dredging*
- 2 tsp salt
- 75 g/3 oz butter, melted

1 Place the yeast and sugar in a small bowl and add 300 ml/½ pt warm water. Stir to dissolve the yeast and sugar. Cover with cling wrap and stand in a warm place for about 15 minutes or until frothy.

2 Place the flour and salt in a large mixing bowl and make a well in the centre. Pour 300 ml/½ pt warm water into the well and add the melted butter and the yeast mixture. Stir to form a sticky dough.

3 Turn the dough out on to a lightly floured surface, adding a little extra flour to the dough if necessary, and knead until smooth and soft. Shape the dough into a ball and place in the cleaned mixing bowl. Cover with cling wrap and stand in a warm place for about 1½ hours or until the dough has doubled in size.

4 Turn the dough out on to a lightly floured surface and knock back to its original size. Allow the dough to rest for about 20 minutes. Meanwhile, dredge three baking sheets with flour.

5 Cut the dough into 12 equal portions and roll each one into a 20-cm/8-in round. Place the rounds on the baking sheets, leaving about 2.5 cm/1 in between them. Cover loosely with cling wrap and return to a warm place to prove again for about 30 minutes.

6 Preheat the oven to 240°C/475°F/Gas 9. Place one of the baking sheets on the bottom of the oven for 3–5 minutes, or until the breads have puffed up. Remove the breads from the baking sheet and place them on the middle oven rack and bake for about 5 minutes, or until firm and just beginning to brown. Place on a warm serving platter and repeat with the remaining pitta breads. Serve warm.

RIGHT
White-washed walls reflect the heat, and such villas as this one near Plakias provide a cool summertime haven.

Sesame Bread Rings

SEMIT

◆ ◆ ◆ ◆

These are the Greek equivalent to pretzels. They may be stored in an airtight container for several days.

Preparation time: about 20 minutes plus proving
Cooking time: about 15 minutes
Oven temperature: 190°C/375°F/Gas 5

MAKES: ABOUT 12

- 450 g/1 lb strong plain flour, plus extra for dredging
- 1 tsp caster sugar
- pinch of salt
- 3 tsp dried yeast
- ½ tsp dried mint
- 150 ml/¼ pt warm water
- 1 egg white mixed with 2 tbsp cold water, to glaze
- sesame seeds, to decorate

1 Place half the flour in a medium-sized bowl with the sugar, salt, dried yeast and mint. Stir in the warm water to make a sticky dough.

2 Using your hands, mix in half the remaining flour, then turn the mixture out on to a lightly floured surface and continue to knead the dough, working in the remaining flour if necessary, until the dough is no longer sticky, but smooth and soft. Return to the cleaned bowl, cover with cling wrap and allow to rest for 5 minutes.

3 Cut the dough into four equal portions. Roll each portion out to a 60 cm/24 in long sausage shape and cut into three smaller sausage shapes of equal length. Shape into rings, moulding the dough together at the join in order to seal.

4 Preheat the oven to 190°C/375°F/Gas 5. Dredge several baking sheets with flour and place the dough rings on them. Cover loosely with cling wrap and prove in a warm place for about 25 minutes.

5 Carefully brush the rings with the egg white mixture and sprinkle heavily with sesame seeds. Bake for about 15 minutes or until crisp and golden. Transfer to a wire rack to cool before serving.

Sesame Rolls

PSOMAKIA ME PROZIMI

◆ ◆ ◆ ◆

These make excellent rolls for all occasions, so freeze whatever you don't need immediately and thaw them a few at a time as you require them.

Preparation time: about 30 minutes plus proving
Cooking time: about 20 minutes
Oven temperature: 180°C/350°F/Gas 4

MAKES: ABOUT 48

- 2 tbsp dried yeast
- 1.6 kg/3½ lb plain flour
- 225 g/8 oz caster sugar
- 65 ml/2½ fl oz warm water
- 600 ml/1 pt milk
- 3 eggs, beaten
- few drops of vanilla essence
- 100 g/4 oz unsalted butter, melted
- vegetable oil, for greasing
- 1 egg, beaten, to glaze
- sesame seeds, to decorate

1 Place the yeast, 3 tbsp flour, ½ tsp sugar, ½ tsp salt and the warm water into a small bowl. Stir until the yeast and sugar have dissolved, then cover with cling wrap and leave in a warm place for about 15 minutes or until frothy.

2 Place the milk in a large mixing bowl and stir in the remaining sugar and salt, the beaten eggs and the vanilla essence. Stir in the frothy yeast mixture and beat well.

3 Sift half of the remaining flour into the mixing bowl and beat well. Add the melted butter and beat, adding the remaining flour, sifting it in as required to make a stiff dough. Turn the dough out on to a lightly floured surface and knead for about 10 minutes or until the dough is smooth and elastic. Return to the cleaned bowl, cover with cling wrap and leave in a warm place for about 1½ hours or until doubled in size.

4 Turn the dough out and knock back to its original size. Return the dough to the bowl, cover, and leave in a warm place for a further hour until risen.

5 Turn the dough out on to a lightly floured surface and knock back to its original size. Divide the dough into about 48 pieces, the size of a walnut. Roll each piece into an 18 cm/7 in sausage shape and twist, tie or coil it into an attractive design for a bread roll. Place the shapes on greased baking sheets and loosely cover with cling wrap. Leave in a warm place for 30 minutes to rise.

6 Preheat the oven to 180°C/350°F/Gas 4. Carefully brush each roll with the beaten egg to glaze and sprinkle generously with sesame seeds. Bake for about 15–20 minutes, in batches if necessary, until the rolls are golden brown, risen and hollow-sounding when tapped underneath. Transfer to a wire rack to cool before serving.

Christmas Bread
CHRISTOPSOMO

◆ ◆ ◆ ◆

This is a traditional recipe made all over Greece at Christmas time. The wife of the house, who bakes the bread, pushes an imprint of her hand into the dough, telling the children that Jesus blessed the loaf while it was baking. If both loaves are not required at the same time, wrap, label and freeze one, allowing several hours for thawing at room temperature when it is required.

Preparation time: about 30 minutes plus proving
Cooking time: about 30 minutes
Oven temperature: 180°C/350°F/Gas 4
MAKES: 2 LOAVES

- 3 tbsp dried yeast
- 375 g/12 oz caster sugar
- 1.6 kg/3½ lb plain flour
- pinch of salt
- 120 ml/4 fl oz warm water
- 5 eggs
- 375 ml/12 fl oz milk
- few drops of vanilla essence
- 225 g/8 oz butter, melted
- 100 g/4 oz dried figs, chopped
- 50 g/2 oz semi-dried apricots, chopped
- 225 g/8 oz blanched almonds, chopped
- 100 g/4 oz sultanas
- finely grated zest of 1 orange
- finely grated zest of 1 lemon
- vegetable oil, for greasing

1 Place the yeast, 1 tsp sugar, 2 tbsp flour, salt and warm water into a small bowl. Stir to dissolve the yeast and sugar, then cover with cling wrap and leave in a warm place for about 15 minutes, or until frothy.

2 In a large mixing bowl, beat together 4 eggs, the remaining sugar and the milk. Stir in the frothy yeast mixture, 700 g/1½ lb of the remaining flour and the vanilla essence. Stir in the melted butter and then the remaining ingredients.

3 Mix to form a stiff dough, then turn out on to a lightly floured surface and knead, with the addition of the remaining flour if necessary, for about 10 minutes or until the dough is soft and smooth.

4 Return the dough to the cleaned mixing bowl and cover with cling wrap. Leave in a warm place to prove for about 1½ hours or until doubled in size. Turn out on to a lightly floured surface and knead the dough back to its original size. Return to the bowl again, cover, and leave in a warm place for a further 30 minutes.

5 Divide the dough into six equal portions. Roll each portion into about a 30 cm/12 in sausage shape and braid

three of them together to form a plait, moulding the ends together to seal. Repeat with the other three sausage shapes to make another plait. Place each braid on a lightly oiled baking sheet, cover loosely with cling wrap and leave in a warm place for a final 30–40 minutes until the bread has risen.

6 Preheat the oven to 180°C/350°F/Gas 4. Beat the remaining egg in a small bowl and use to glaze both braids. Bake the bread for about 30 minutes, or until golden and hollow-sounding when tapped underneath. Transfer to a wire rack to cool before serving.

Easter Bread
TSOUREKI

$\diamond$ $\diamond$ $\diamond$ $\diamond$

This rich dough bread is traditionally eaten at Easter time. The red egg symbolizes the blood of Christ and is made by boiling it in water mixed with red dye and vinegar, allowing it to cool, then using it as directed in the recipe.

Preparation time: about 1 hour plus proving
Cooking time: about 45 minutes
Oven temperature: 190°C/375°F/Gas 5
MAKES: 1 LOAF

- *300 ml/½ pt lukewarm milk*
- *3 tsp dried yeast*
- *900 g/2 lb strong plain flour*
- *175 g/6 oz caster sugar*
- *pinch of salt*
- *finely grated zest of ½ orange*
- *finely grated zest of ½*

- *lemon*
- *50 g/2 oz unsalted butter, cubed, plus extra for greasing*
- *3 eggs, well beaten*
- *2 tsp vanilla essence*
- *3 eggs, dyed red (optional)*
- *1 egg yolk mixed with 3 tbsp milk, to glaze*

1 Place the milk in a large bowl and sprinkle the yeast over it. Stir until dissolved, then add 225 g/8 oz of the flour and 25 g/1 oz of the sugar. Cover with cling wrap and place in a warm place for about 1 hour, or until the mixture is frothy.

2 In another large bowl, sift together the remaining flour, sugar and salt. Stir in the orange and lemon zest

and rub in the butter until the mixture resembles very fine breadcrumbs. Make a well in the centre of the flour mixture and pour in the frothy yeast, beaten eggs and vanilla essence. Stir until a dough forms.

3 Turn the mixture out on to a lightly floured surface and knead for 10–15 minutes, or until the dough is very soft and elastic. Return to the cleaned bowl, cover with cling wrap and allow to prove in a warm place for 1–2 hours, or until doubled in size.

4 Turn the dough out on to a lightly floured surface and knead it back to its original size. Divide the dough into three equal portions and roll each portion into a 30-cm/12-in sausage shape. Lay the sausage shapes side-by-side and pinch them together at one end. Plait the strips of dough, pinching them together at the finishing end. Form the braid into a ring and pinch the join together in order to seal.

5 Press the red eggs, if using, into the dough and place the loaf on a buttered baking sheet. Cover with cling wrap and leave in a warm place for about 2 hours or until doubled in size. Meanwhile, pre-heat the oven to 190°C/375°F/Gas 5.

6 Remove the cover, carefully brush the loaf with the egg yolk and milk glaze and bake for 40–45 minutes or until golden and hollow-sounding when tapped underneath. Transfer to a wire rack to cool.

Index